THE JOURNEY
OF THE SITAR IN
INDIAN CLASSICAL MUSIC

THE JOURNEY
OF THE SITAR IN
INDIAN CLASSICAL MUSIC

Origin, History, and Playing Styles

DR. SWARN LATA

iUniverse, Inc.
Bloomington

The Journey of the Sitar in Indian Classical Music
Origin, History, and Playing Styles

iUniverse books may be ordered through booksellers or by contacting:

iUniverse
1663 Liberty Drive
Bloomington, IN 47403
www.iuniverse.com
1-800-Authors (1-800-288-4677)

ISBN: 978-1-4759-4706-9 (sc)
ISBN: 978-1-4759-4708-3 (hc)
ISBN: 978-1-4759-4707-6 (ebk)

Printed in the United States of America

iUniverse rev. date: 02/06/2013

Contents

To my mother Sheela, and, father, Late Krishan Chand

PREFACE

This book discusses in-depth the sitar, a stringed, plucked instrument of India, with particular reference to the sitar's place in Indian classical music. I explore its origin, structure, changing *vaadan shailies,* and practical techniques relating to the instrument's structure. I have attempted to search out how the continuity of tradition has been maintained by bringing out the similarities between the modern instrument and the earliest musical instruments, such as old veenas and their variants. This work is primarily a survey of origin of the sitar, styles of different *Gharanas,* and the techniques of playing with reference to their historical evolution. I have attempted to follow the evolution of the instruments on the basis of descriptions in Sanskrit and other texts from earlier times. Representations of instruments in sculptures and paintings from the various historical periods provided supplementary information.

As far as it is known, this field has generally remained unexplored. While Dr. Lal Mani Mishra has worked on different varieties of Indian musical instruments, I have confined myself to the study of only the sitar, the plucked variety of stringed instrument used in Hindustani classical music. I was fascinated by different instruments in my childhood, but I loved the sitar the most. So I took this subject and proceeded. I collected the materials and necessary information pertaining to this work from various universities, institutions, libraries, museums, temples, ancient monuments catalogued in the Archaeological Survey of India, eminent sitar players, and musicologists.

ACKNOWLEDGMENTS

I offer my humble obeisance to God Almighty for providing me the mental courage and physical strength to finish this work. I owe my sincere thanks and gratitude to Dr. Saroj Ghosh, my guide, for her valuable scholarly guidance when I was doing my PhD. She provided me with many valuable materials and much necessary information.

I am very much thankful to the library staffs of Punjabi University, Patiala, Shimla University, Kurukshetra University, and Delhi University. I do not have enough words to thank the library and office staff of the Department of Music, Panjab University, Chandigarh, which provided full cooperation and supplied the relevant material whenever required.

My gratitude is due to Shri Buddhadittya Mukerjee, Shujaat Hussain Khan Sahib, Shri Gopal Krishan, Ustaad Vilayat Khan Sahib, Debu Prasaad Chakarborthy, Mohsin Ali Khan Sahib, Piare Lal, and Salil Shankar, who spared their precious time for interviews during my research work.

I thank my brother, Dr. Anant, for his moral support, and Vijay, who arranged interviews with Dr. C. Lawrence House and Dr. David Kaplin, Department of Music, University at Saskatoon, Canada, when I visited Saskatoon in regard to my research. Dr. Kaplin was really nice to take me to his personal museum of instruments, where I took pictures of instruments of the sitar family.

I give my sincere thanks to my parents, who always encouraged and helped me to pursue my studies.

I would like to thank my daughters, Geetika, and Ritu for understanding my long nights with a pile of books around me, searching for the answers to my questions. I love them for their faithful support and for bearing the difficulties of life with me. They are my inspiration.

Words cannot express my gratitude to my editorial team at iUniverse for their professional advice and assistance in polishing my manuscript. The list of helpers is long, and I express my gratitude to all.

INTRODUCTION

The work embodied in this book has been divided into six chapters. Each chapter has further been divided into subcategories. The book will take the reader through an evolutionary journey of the sitar. The origin of the sitar goes back to the thirteenth century on the basis of the *tri-tantri veena* of Ameer Khusro. As change is the law of nature, this instrument went through many changes. The development of sitar techniques may be traced to a number of sources—the *bin, rabab, dhrupad ang, khayal ang,* vocal music, and other instruments. Of these sources, the most important seems to have been the veena. During the eighteenth and nineteenth centuries, sitar techniques developed to a great extent, and a unique system originated of raga *prastaar,* known as *gat shaily.* Previously, the sitar was used as an accompaniment or gap-filler for vocal music. Gradually, the right-hand technique grew with enlarged *mizraab bols.* Then, the left hand started showing its capacity with *swara vistaars, meend* work, elaborations, *kan-swara, gamak, ghaseet,* and the sitar became a full-fledged instrument, having the capacity to depict the chirping of the birds, burst of clouds, waterfalls, and all the nine *rasas* of Indian music. Creative compositions by great *ustaads* have made this instrument a favorite of millions in India as well as in foreign countries.

Compositions for the sitar have also gone through vast changes. Every *ustaad* has composed *gats* to his own taste and in his own name, such as Ameer Khani *gat,* Raza Khani *gat,* Maseet Khani *gat,* Zafar Khani *gat,* and others. Maseet Khani, Raza Khani, and Imdad Khani *gats* are the most popular, easy, and attractive *gats.* For *swara vistaar* and *raga vistaar,* the right- and left-hand techniques have played the most important roles, and flourishing artists of the sitar continue to experiment.

The first chapter deals with the meaning of music, its origin, kinds of music, *swaras,* old and new, light and classical music, and the importance of music.

The second chapter is a historical survey of old veenas. First of all, I describe the meaning of musical instruments. There are hundreds of instruments in the world. They must be classified; otherwise, one cannot differentiate them. For this purpose, I have shown musical instruments under four categories: *Tat Vadhyas, Sushir Vadhyas, Avnadh,* and *Ghan Vadhyas.* I cover the stringed instruments of Vedic and ancient periods in this chapter and discuss the historical background of stringed instruments. I trace the structure of old veenas, their *vaadan shaily,* and the evolution of veenas from ancient times, as well as covering the modification of veenas.

Chapter 3 is a detailed historical survey that traces the origin of the sitar and includes pictures of instruments from one-stringed to thirteen-stringed, which I have collected from various library books, museums, and art galleries. I have searched for *swaras* of Vedic, ancient, and modern periods and for the tuning systems. My research includes *vaadan shaily* from olden times to present. For this purpose, I consulted books on world history that tell the traditions, living methods, art, sculpture, paintings, music, and musical instruments of almost all the countries of the world. To find the place of origin of the sitar and by whom it was invented, I had to study vast literature, including Hindu scriptures—*Ramayan, Mahabharta,* and *Upanishads*—as well as books on Western music, and the entire history of music had to be traced.

What were the *swaras* in the Vedic and ancient periods and what *swaras* are used in the modern period? The changes in basic *swaras* and their development, *shruties* and their division, and *gram* from the ancient as well as modern periods have been covered as the passage of time changed the forms of the sitar. I have searched for different types of sitars and their prevailing structure in different periods.

The structural form of the sitar, its playing position, *mizraab* strokes, and, most importantly, care of the instrument all are covered under one roof in this chapter.

Chapter 4 describes in detail the systematic approach to *vaadan shailies* of the sitar. I have covered the famous sitar players who have contributed toward the progress and development of sitar *vaadan.* A historical survey of changing *mizraab* strokes has also been included, as well as changing techniques of *Jhala* playing. I have researched basic techniques of playing sitar Khani, Zaafar Khani, Ameer Khani, and Imdad Khani *gat shailies*. Unfortunately, no recordings of old sitar players are available, although some written records have been preserved and collected.

Chapter 5 traces the evolution and origin of *Gharana* and its meaning and current existence. A section of the chapter deals with *gats* of different *laya* with different *bols*, and it covers changing *vaadan shailies* of different *Gharanas*.

Chapter 6 describes the place of sitar in Indian classical music, its use in almost all the musical functions, and its future.

The entire presentation is like a garland linking one chapter to another. Besides my own research work, there are thoughts of various authors and poets given as quotations from the original sources. These are identified in my text, and I give more formal citations in my bibliography.

The oldest detailed exposition of musical theory that has survived the ravages of time is found in the treatise entitled *Natya Shastra*, written by Bharat. Others are *Sangeet Ratnakar*, by Pt. Sharangdev; *Sangeet Parizuat*, by Pt. Ahobal; and *Rag Vibodh*, by Somraj.

CHAPTER 1

The Meaning of Music

Because human beings live in societies based on mutual ideas and actions, they must possess some medium that can express and exchange their feelings. Like language, music has been a source of such expressions from the very ancient times.

Music is the pride of our Indian culture and is based on scientific principles.

What is a musical instrument? While one can attempt to give an answer, however vague, the query itself implies others: What is music? What is the origin of music? What are the ancient forms?

Swami Prajnanand wrote in his 1973 book, *Historical Development of Indian Music*: "Music, the English word, is a derivative from French word *muse*."

In Latin, the term is *musica*. In Sanskrit, it is called *gana, giti*, or *sangeet*. The later treatises on music have explained or rather defined *sangeet* as the combination of vocal music, drumming, and dance (*geet, vadhya*, and *nritya*).

Pt. Sharangdev wrote in his book, *Sangeet Ratnakar*: "Geetam Vadhyam tatha Nrityam Triyam Sangeet muchyate."

The three forms vocal music, instrumental, and dance combined together are called sangeet.

Pt. Ahobal wrote in his book, *Sangeet Parizaat*: "Geetam Vaditre Nrityam Triyam Sangeet muchyate."

Indian music, or *sangeet,* comprises three arts: gayan, *vaadan*, and *nritya. Sangeet* is a technical term, used for vocal and instrumental music, along with the art of dance.

The Origin of Music

The Indian form of music is one of the oldest in the world, as is evident from historical facts about India.

According to Swami Abhenananda, writing in his 1968 book *India and Her People*: "If we read the writings and historical accounts left by Pliny, Strabo, Magasthanese, Herodotus (who lived in the Vth century B.C.), Prophyry and a host of other ancient authors of different countries, we shall see, how highly the civilization of India was regarded by them."

In fact, between the years 1500 BC and 500 BC, the Hindus were so advanced in religion, metaphysics, philosophy, science, art, music, and medicine that no other nation could stand as their rival or compete with them in any of these branches of knowledge.

To find out the history of a topic, one has to collect historical information and facts and go deeply into the roots of the matter. It is the duty of the historian not to let that past be forgotten. He or she should trace these gifts back to their sources, give them their due place in the time scheme, and show how they influenced or prepared the ground for the succeeding ages. It is important to discover what portion of present-day Indian life and thought is the distinctive contribution of each race or creed that has lived in this land.

To discover the origin of music, I studied a vast literature on Indian music.

In no other art, science, or other department of human activity has the doctrine of evolution been so enthusiastically welcomed, so eagerly adopted, and so wholeheartedly endorsed, as in music.

Writing of the remote origins of music in *Vishwa Sangeet Ka Itihas*, Amal Dash Sharma maintained: "Vocal efforts may have originated in imitation of the cries of the animals, which were mimicked, but of the origin of the musical instruments, it is difficult to speak with certainty."

The first sound produced by the human throat was musical. The vibrations of vocal chords created sound. The main property of music is sound or *naad*. The *naad* is unchangeable.

The view of Erwin Felber, expressed in his book *The Indian Music of the Vedic and the Classical Periods*, was that: "Speech and music have descended from a common origin in a primitive language, which was neither speaking nor singing, but something both."

Music is a science in which laws are fixed and invariable. Just like two plus two is four in the West as well as in the East, the fundamental laws of music are also permanent for all people of all ages. Even now, *naad* is considered to be the basis of music.

In his book *Natya Shastra*, Bharat discussed the *atodhya vidhi* in which he has explained the human body as the *shariri* veena, because vocal chords function as strings: "So our throat is the most beautiful and sweet instrument."

It is written in our Hindu Vedas that, when the universe came into existence, Brahma created music and gave it as a gift to Lord Mahadeva, who then gave it to Devi Saraswati, who became the goddess of music, and people worshipped her as veena *pustak dharini*.

The excavations in Mohenjodaro and Harappa have brought to light the place of music in ancient and prehistoric periods and show the high status of music at those times. Many valuable objects, such as seals, sacred tanks, dolls of the deities, and musical instruments like crude types of flutes, lutes, and veenas, have been found. These veenas were stringed instruments having structures for seven notes.

The Vedas are the most important fundamentals of all wisdom. They are the basic *granths* of Aryans written in Sanskrit and are storehouses of the knowledge in every aspect of social and cultural life of the people of that time. We come to know from Vedas that Narad, the son of Brahma, invented the veena, a stringed instrument, which became very much popular in those days.

Besides *Vedic sangeet, gandharav sangeet* was prevalent. It enjoyed a special place in the field of Indian music. Vedic music was formalized as it followed rules and methods. The name Gandharav was given to a great musician. A methodical system had already been worked out before the age of Panini, who lived about 600 BC. This methodology was adopted by Persians, Greeks, Arabs, and by Europeans too.

In the Vedic period, the scale of four notes known as *swarantra* came into existence, although the actual, precise origin of Vedic music cannot be traced.

An account of the well-known seven notes *Ma, Ga, Re, Sa, Ni, Dha, Pa,* whose equivalents are still in use in our present-day music, is found for the first time in Mandukiya Shiksha of *Atharva Veda.* It is clearly mentioned there that the *Samveda* hymns were sung on the notes known as:

"Shadaj	—	Sa
Rishabh	—	Re
Gandhar	—	Ga
Madhyam	—	Ma
Pancham	—	Pa
Dhaiwat	—	Dha
Nishad	—	Ni"

According to Mandukiya Shiksha, Atharav ved:

"Shadaj Rishabh Gandharan
Madhyam Panchmsttha
Dhaiwateshach Nishadashach
Swara Sapteh Samsu"

The seven notes: Shadaj, Rishabh, Gandhar, Madhayam, Pancham, Dhaiwat and Nishad come from Samved.

Deb Asheesh writes in his book, *Quiz on Indian Music and Dance*:

"Shadaj is produced by - Peacock
Rishabh is produced by - Cow
Gandhar is produced by - Goat
Madhyam is produced by - Heron
Pancham is produced by - Koyal
Dhaiwat is produced by - Horse
Nishad is produced by - Elephant"

In the *Yajur Veda*, the notes were called:

Udata - Raised - *Komal/* High Tones
Anudata - Not raised (Grave)
Swarit - Harmonic *Swaras* (circumflex)
Nishaad and *Gandhaar* - Udata swaras
Rishabh and *Dhaiwat* - Anudata swaras
Shadaj, Madhayam and *Pancham-Swarit*

Narad wrote in his book, *Nardiya Shiksha:* "According to *Samveda*, the seven notes are:

Vedic Notes				Laukik Notes		English
1.	*Prathama*	*Ga*	First	—	*Ma*	—	F
2.	*Dvitlya*	*Re*	Second	—	*Ga*	—	E
3.	*Tritiya*	*Sa*	Third	—	*Re*	—	D
4.	*Chaturtha*	*Ni*	Fourth	—	*Sa*	—	C
5.	*Atiswara*	*Dha*	Extreme note	—	*Ni*	—	B
6.	*Mandra*	*Pa*	Sixth	—	*Dha*	—	A
7.	*Krusta*	*Ma*	Pulled	—	*Pa*	—	G"

The expert singers and chanters of the Vedic age knew very well the specific laws and methods of application of the three registers: bass, medium, and high; that is, *Mandra, Madhya,* and *Taar.* The three ancient register notes, or *sthanswaras,* were raised, not raised, and balancing circumflex. These three—known as *udata, unudata,* and *swarit*—came to be used as three kinds of pitches of speaking, as well as of singing voices. Rhythm and tempo were used in accordance with different types of feet of the Vedic meters: *gayatri, Jagati, anustupa,* etc. The time measure or *tala* was observed in hymnal songs and in different types of *samgaan* in two different ways, with beat and without beat. Clapping of hands used to be the method for time measuring a song, along with hand waving or different movements of limbs of the body.

So, after a deep study, one comes to know that the origin of music or *sangeet* is traced back to the Vedic period.

Ancient Forms of Music

In the ancient times, music was divided into two categories: *Margi sangeet* and *Deshi sangeet.*

Margi sangeet is believed to have been originated by Brahma, who taught this art to Bharat muni. *Margi sangeet* was sung by *Gandharvas* only and was known as *Achal sangeet.* Its main aim was God realization, whereas *Deshi sangeet* aimed at recreation for people. It was the changed style of *Margi sangeet. Deshi sangeet* had no hard and fast rules, so it flourished the most.

In *gayan* as well as in *vaadan, Deshi sangeet* achieved a great place, because it was sung or played according to the tastes of the people. The sitar is such an instrument, which has kept the old as well as modern traditions alive. One can play light as well as classical music on it, so it is a perfect instrument, which embraces light tunes of *Deshi sangeet, thumris,* and classical ragas as well.

Classification of Music

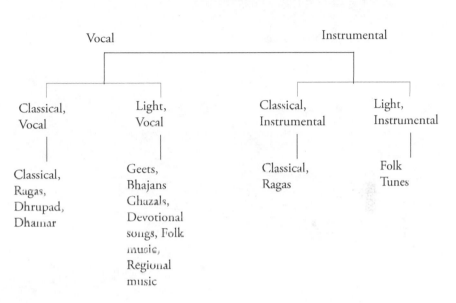

Music, or *sangeet,* can be classified into two categories: vocal music and instrumental music. Vocal music is known as *gayan,* or singing. It includes all types of songs, ranging from light folk tunes, light devotional songs, patriotic songs, *geets, ghazals, thumri, tappa, dadra,* and seasonal songs to classical *dhrupads,* classical devotional *bhajans,* and classical ragas of all seasons, moods, and times, such as morning, afternoon, and night ragas.

In classical instrumental music, one can play classical ragas of all times and moods. The light instrumental music includes various tunes—*thumri, kehrawa* beat tunes, regional folk *dhuns, tappa,* and more. The instrument can be used in an orchestra. Pt. Ravi Shankar ji played *tukras* on the sitar with his orchestra in 1960 in New York City. The result was audience appreciation that came like a cloud burst.

Light music, or *khayal,* has two parts: *sthai* and *antra.* The compositions can be played with fast beats or slow beats, which are called *Drut gats* and *Vilambit gats.* Light music comes from classical music, because when the artist practices classical music, he discovers some light notes that are soothing to the heart and console the mind. The light compositions are related to our daily routine, whereas classical music is bound by its rules.

Light music can be played with sweetness of melody, keeping in view the rhythmic conditions. Classical light music includes all the nine *rasas*, which depict the different human emotions.

Nine *Rasas* in Indian Music

1. *Shringar ras* — feeling of love

2. *Hasya ras* — feeling of happiness

3. *Karuna ras* — feeling of sadness

4. *Veer ras* — feeling of heroism

5. *Raudra ras* — feeling of terror

6. *Bhayankar ras* — feeling of awfulness

7. *Vibhatsa ras* — feeling of panic

8. *Adbhut ras* — feeling of strangeness

9. *Shant ras* — feeling of quietness

Classical music has some limitations. Only classical ragas are allowed to be sung or played and must be in accord with the set rules, but light music can be of any kind, as I have explained in the chart showing the classification of music.

In light music, one can imagine the emotions and can depict them by playing small *alankars* or using *khatka, murki, gamak,* and *meend*, which increase the beauty of the raga or any other composition. Classical ragas can be played or sung with much effect in expressing the emotional aspects as well as the purity of the raga.

The Importance of Music

The significance of music can be understood from the famous two premptory dictums in Hindu scriptures. There is no knowledge beyond the knowledge of music.

God himself is personified as *"Naad-Brahma"* and music as divine. It is a gift of the Almighty and the highest among the Fourteen *Vidyas* and the Sixty-Four *Kalas* enumerated in our holy scriptures. *Vidya* means knowing about the various spheres of knowledge and thus leads to the goal of God realization. *Kala* refers to all other branches of knowledge, which help human beings to lead happy and satisfied lives.

Indian music depicts emotions of life and creates harmony and poise in everyday life. It is purely a melodic art devoid of any harmonized accompaniment other than a drone. The art of music of India exists only under cultivated patronage and in its own intimate environment. It is the chamber music of an aristocratic society, in which the patron retains the musicians for his own entertainment and for the pleasure of his friends, or it is temple music in which the musician is the servant of God.

Music is called the fifth Veda, as it is considered to be of divine origin and thus is worshipped and regarded as sacred. Music has been seen almost universally as the purest form of art, because it combines and assimilates all together in one art, beauty, delight, and love. Music is the *"Sarvottam Sooksham Kala,"* or best among all the fine arts. All arts aspire to the condition of music. It is the most direct expression of beauty. It serves as the constant companion of human beings from birth to death, since there is no ceremony or occasion in society when music is not present to accompany those precious moments of existence. It is an essential spiritual art and is the language of the soul. Music is the best medium of communication. It is spontaneous expression and holy communion with the divine. The language of music is melody, harmony, and rhythm, which bring to our lives the highest gift of culture.

Music is said to be the speech of angels. The man who has no music in himself or is unmoved by a concord of sweet sounds is fit for treasons, stratagems, and spoils.

CHAPTER 2

Stringed Instruments

What Is a Musical Instrument?

Most broadly put, an instrument is any material used for producing sound in music. The oldest instrument is the human body, which has been called the *Gatra* veena. "Veena" is a word used for some specific *tat vadhya* or stringed instrument, such as *Matt Kokila, Vipanchi*, or *Ek-tantri* veena. On the other hand, *tat vadhya* is also referred to as veena—that is, an instrument that has *tat* or *tantri,* can be called a veena. When we refer to *tat vadhyas*, we mean veenas.

Classification of Musical Instruments

The oldest detailed exposition of musical theory that has survived the ravages of time is found in the treatise entitled *Natya Shastra,* written by Bharat. The twenty-eighth chapter of this *grantha* deals with *shruti, swara, gram, taal*, and other matters. This book tells the story of four types of *musical instruments*: *tat, sushir, avnadh*, and *ghan vadhyas.*

Indian musical instruments have a very important place in our day-to-day life. These have been organized under four categories:

- *Tat vadhyas*
- *Sushir vadhyas*
- *Avnadh vadhyas*
- *Ghan vadhyas*

Tat Vadhyas: These are the stringed instruments that produce *swaras*, when plucked by a *mizraab* or plectrum. *Tat vadhyas* are also of two types: *tat* and *vitat vadhyas*. The first category consists of the sitar, the *tanpura*, and the sarod, which are played with the help of fingers and a plectrum or *mizraab*. The second category includes *sarangi, bella, israj*, and others, which are played with the help of bow. *Tat vadhyas* are called chordophones in English.

Sushir Vadhyas: These are pipe-like wind instruments, blown by the mouth either by full or half breath. The flute, *nafeeri, poongi, shehnai, been*, clarinet, mouth-organ, and more, all come under this category.

Avnadh Vadhyas: The instruments that are made of skins stretched over a hollow circular form at one end are called *avnadh vadhyas*. The tabla, *pakhawaj, nagara, damru, mridang* all are of the *Avnadh Vadhya* family.

Ghan Vadhyas: The instruments that are struck by the hand or a wooden stick are called *ghan vadhyas*. Metal bells, *ghadial, mazeera, jhanj, kartal, Jal-tarang*, and *kushat-trang* are in this category.

I am of the opinion that instead of four categories, the above-mentioned instruments should be divided into two groups only:

1. Instruments relating to *swara*.
2. Instruments relating to *Tal-laya* or rhythm.

Instruments under this first category are: veena, sitar, *tanpura, bela*, sarod, flute, *shehnai*, harmonium, piano, *Jal-tarang, kasht-tarang*, and other similar instruments.

The second category consists of tabla, *pakhawaj*, drum, *dhol, majeera, Jhanj, kartal*, and others.

Stringed Instruments of the Vedic and Ancient Periods (Historical Survey)

Historians differ greatly on how to define the Vedic period. Some consider it to be as old as 6600 BC, but according to another group, it is no older than 3100 BC. However, all agree that Vedas are our basic *granths*, in whichever period they might have been written.

Samveda is musical in form and nature. It is a compilation of the *shalokas* or mantras of *Rigveda*. These *shalokas* or mantras were sung and the tamburist played the *tambura*. This process of singing or this technique of mantra singing was called *samgaan*. "*Sa*" means *prana,* and "*am*" means energy in Sanskrit. "*Gann*" means "*gatha.*" *Samgaan* was known as the medium through which songs (*gans*) in praise of gods and goddesses were accompanied by a veena, which means that stringed instruments existed in that period also.

As Swami Prajnanada has written in *The Historical Development of Music*: "In samgaan, an instrument called 'Vaan' or 'Venu' was played. It had seven *swara*s, namely:

1. Krushtha (Krusta)
2. Prathma
3. Dvitiya
4. Tritiya
5. Chaturatha
6. Mandra
7. Atiswara

He added, "The word 'van' seems to have been derived from its fore runner 'vana' which means sound. 'Van' conveyed the idea of sound and musical tone."

These seven notes were *Ma, Ga, Re, Sa, Ni, Dha, Pa*. The other names for these seven notes were:

1. *Udaat: Nishaad and Gandhaar were called udaat swaras*
2. *Anudaat: Rishabh and Dhaiwat were called anudaat swaras*
3. *Swarit: Shadaj, Madhyam and Pancham were called swarit swaras.*

The *munis* or the musicians of that period gave new names to these *swaras*:

1. *Shadaj*
2. *Rishabh*
3. *Gandhaar*
4. *Madhyam*
5. *Pancham*
6. *Dhaiwat*
7. *Nishaad*

We learn about the *tat* or stringed instruments from the great *granth Hiranyakeshi sutra*. This book contains the names of *talluck* veena, *kand* veena, *pichhora, alabu* veena, *kapisheerash* veena, and more. *Gatra* veena was very popular in the Vedic period. We get brief information about the instruments popular in those days from the *Upnishads* and *samhitas*. Kaand veena is described in *Kathak Samhitas* (*Manu samriti granth*), and we come across *maruud* veena in *Rigveda Sanhita*. Another name for veena was *vaan*. It was played with the help of a *Nakhi*, which was worn on the first finger of the right hand. Nowadays, this is known as a *mizraab*. We get the description of *shat tantri* veena in *Shankhayan Shuraut Sutra*, written by Kapil Muni.

In *samgaan, alabu* veenas, and *sheel* veenas were played. *Alabu* veena's name comes in Panini's book: *Paniniya Shiksha, Shalok No. 23*. The *Gatra* veena used to be played in the *Sam gana* before the sacrificial altar and the *daarvi* veena to the accompaniment of *Jati-raga-gana*. The *Gatra* even had seven strings. The method of playing this veena was just like the harp and lyre of the Western countries.

Stringed Instruments in the Ancient Period

While studying *Ramayan* and *Mahabharata*, I came across variety of stringed instruments of that period.

The *Ramayan* (Indian religious book, 400 BC) describes the oldest veena, named *Vipanchi*. *Gandharav sangeet* was popular in *Ramayan Yug*. Veena *vaadan* was done as solo as well as to accompany the *gandharav gaan*.

In the *Mahabharta* period, the following veenas were popular:

1. *Adambar* veena
2. *Analambi* veena
3. *Amrat Kundali*
4. *Alabu* veena
5. *Alapani* veena—The description of *alapani* veena is found in *Sangeet Ratnakar, Sangeet Samyasaar, Sangeet Sudha,* and other books.
6. *Ek-tantri* veena—The *Ek-tantri* had only one string and was played with a twelve-inch long *shalaka*. We can say that *Ek-tantri* is the mother of all veenas. It is said that Lav and Kush used the *Ek-tantri* veena in *Ramayan gatha*.

    Ghoshwati, ghoshak, and *brahma* veena are also names for *Ek-tantri* veena, which was popular from the seventh century to the thirteenth century. All the books related to music written in this period describe the *Ek-tantri* veena in detail.

    Some of the famous writers of this period were Someshwar, Sharangdev, and Sudha kalash.

    One instrument, *Ek-tara*, was a small *Ek-tantri* veena that was played by plucking with a fingernail to produce a sweet sound while singing.

    The players of *Ek-tantri* veena produced all *swaras* on one string only, but they achieved full perfection in *swaras*.
7. *Kachchapi* veena—This instrument is described in *Natya Shastra*, written by Bharat. The guard of this veena was flattened, and the rest of the shape was just like an *Ek-tantri* veena. It had two strings and was played with two fingers of the right hand.
8. *Kaand* veena—This veena's name comes from *Kaathak Sanhita*.
9. *Kalawati* veena—This veena was referred to in *Vadhya Parkash,* written by Pt. Vidhya Vilasi, but the writer gave no clue to the playing techniques or its shape. It is only an assumption that, because it is listed in veenas, so it might have one or two strings like other veenas.
10. *Katyayni* veena—Pt. Vidhya Vilasi has given a reference to this veena in his book *Vidhya Parkash,* written in 1780.
11. *Kinnari* veena—The description of this veena is found in *Sangeet Ratnakar* and *Sangeet Saar*. This veena had two strings and

fourteen frets. The musicians of this period set two octaves on the fingerboard and plucked the strings with the first finger of the right hand.

Matang Muni was the inventor of the *Kinnari* veena. There were no frets on any veena before Matang. He originated this technique and put fourteen to eighteen frets on the fingerboard.

A *Kinnari* veena that is exhibited in the Calcutta Museum has three strings, is thirty-five feet long, and has three guards. The stringed instruments of those days had shapes developed from the *Ek-tantri* and *Kinnari* veena.

12. *Kubzika* veena—A little reference to this veena is given in *Vadhya Parkash*, by Pt. Vidhya Vilasi, *Sangeet Makrand*, by Narda, and *Sangeet Sudha*, by Pt. Raghunath. There is no description of its playing techniques or the shape of the instrument.

13. *Koormi* veena—The books *Sangeet Sudha* and *Sangeet Makrand* mention the name of this veena. The book *Vadhya Parkash* also gives a small description of this veena.

14. *Maha Natak* veena—There is in the Karnataka Academy of Music one veena, named *Maha Natak* Veena, which has seven strings. The shape of this veena is like the *Tanjauri* veena. The playing technique is the same as that of the *Ek-tantri* veena, which has no frets. The *Batta been* is the child of the *Tanjauri* veena or the *Ek-tantri* veena. The only difference is that of strings.

15. *Ghoshwati* veena—Maharishi Bharat explained this veena in his book *Natya Shastra*. All the *sangeetacharyas* agree that the *Ek-tantri* and *Ghoshwati* veenas are the same in shape and size. The only difference is that of strings. The *Ek-tantri* veena had only one string, whereas the *Ghoshwati* veena had nine strings. The *vaadak,* or the player, used only the first string to produce resonant sounds and the others were just sympathetic strings, which when plucked produced sweet sounds.

16. *Tambur* veena—There are controversies regarding the place of origin of the *tumbur*, but it must be admitted for many reasons that this instrument originated on the soil of India, and it evolved from the *Ek-tantri* veena. The artists of Indian music gradually developed the finger-plucked, simple *Ek-tantri* veena into the four-stringed *tumbur* veena. Like Narda, Tumbru was a *Gandharav* and this veena is connected with his name. This *Tambur* veena

developed to have four strings and became the *Tambura* in the fourteenth century, and then the name *"Tanpura"* was given to this instrument.

17. *Chitra* veena —Another form was the *Chitra* veena; the great *granth Natya Shastra* gives a description of this instrument. According to Bharat, it had seven strings and was played with the index finger of the right hand. It was very popular in the fifth century.

Until the seventh century, *Vipanchi, Chitra, Ghoshwati,* and *Shat tantri* veenas prevailed.

Changes in Stringed Instruments

I find that stringed instruments reflect these developments:

1. The instrument that seems to be like a harp is *Vipanchi* veena (*Nav-tantri*).
2. The present sarod seems a descendant of the *Chitra* veena (*Sapat-tantri*).
3. The *Ek-tara* has a shape that seems to be derived from the *Ghoshwati* veena or *Ek-tantri* veena. The emergence of the sitar can be traced back to the *Chitra* veena, which had seven strings.
4. The *Swar-mandal* had also seven strings, which is described in *Sangeet Saar*.

Some knowledge is gained from illustrations in caves, temples, and stupas that show *Ek-tantri, Tamburu* veena, *Ghoshwati* or *EK- tara* instruments. However, the artists created the images from their imaginations, so we can't say that they depicted the exact shapes of the instruments. It is not necessary that an artist or a sculpturist should have full knowledge of all the musical instruments. There may be many mistakes in the illustrations of the exact strings, shapes, pegs, and other details.

Although we see a *Vipanchi* veena with nine strings and a *Chitra* veena with seven strings, no clear information is given about the tuning and techniques of these veenas.

In the *Natya Shastra*, there is no description of five- or six-stringed veenas, but we can well imagine from the pictures of sculptures with five or six strings that those images were created with artistic sense, and the pegs on the actual instruments were not at the angles as shown in the pictures.

The *Rabab,* derived from the *Chitra* veena, became popular in sixteenth century. After some changes, it took the name of *sursingar* and then became the sarod. H. A. Popley in his book, *Music of India,* maintains "Tansen is said to be the inventor of Rabab, he made it on the basis of Tambura and Sehtar."

The *Tri-tantri* veena had three strings. The veena that Samrat Chandergupta Vikrmaditya played was the same one. It is the same veena that Amir Khusro got from somewhere and named it *Sehtaar,* because 'Seh' means three and '*taar*' means string, hence the name. Though actually it was a *Tritantri* veena, but Amir Khusro gave it the name of *Seh-taar* in his own Persian language.

The veena that was dominant in Sharangdev's time, the *Tri-tantri* veena, was called *Jantar* also by the people of that period, and it is known as the mother of the sitar.

In his book, *Sitar and Its Techniques,* Dev Vratt Chaudhary's opinion is that sitar is the modification of Tritantri veena.

Pandit Sharangdev wrote in his book *Sangeet Ratnakar:* "Tatta Tritantrikaive loke, Jantra Shabdenochyate."

The three-stringed instrument was called by the name of Jantra.

Dandi veena's description is given in the book *Sangeet Parijaat,* written by Ahobal Pandit. It also had three strings. Its gourd was on its left side, because the tradition to keep the gourd on one's shoulder while playing was very popular.

According to Harinayaka Suri, in his book *Sangeet Saar:* "Sometimes, it was burdensome to play in this position, so the veena was modified to some extent. The gourd was fitted to the right side, so that it could stand on the floor and was easy to play. The veena player could sit easily with folded legs and keep the veena before him on the ground. This tradition came into existence in the thirteenth century."

Besides the above mentioned veenas and stringed instruments, we learn about the additional veenas from the study of *Raag Vibodh,* written by Som Nath, one of the most valuable of ancient treatises that have been preserved for us in a useful form. There is no copy of this *granth,* but the work is mentioned by Sir William Jones in his book, *The Musical Instruments.*

"The second chapter of Raga Vibodh deals with the minute details of different veenas with rules of playing them. These are Veenottama, Brahma veena, Kailash veena, Sarang veena, Kooram veena, Akaash veena, Bharag veena, Ravna veena, Gauri veena, Ambika veena, Baan veena, Kashayap veena, Savayambhu veena, Bhujang veena, Bhog veena, Kinner veena, Tri swari veena, Saraswati veena, Mauli veena, Manoratha veena, Gannath veena, Ravasia-Hastha veena, Chitrika, Natya Nagrik Veena, Kumbhika, Adambari, Tantri Sagar and Ambun Veena."

Acharya Brahapati writes in his book, *Bhartiya Sangeet Ke Itihas Ka Pracheen Kaal*, "The Brahma veena was made by God Brahma and was played with a twelve finger long shalaka. There were no frets, and only one string. This is known as the 'mother of all the veenas.'"

There is a story that after Brahma, God Shankar made an instrument named *Analambi* veena, but a research scholar should always doubt the sayings of others. A shop in a village can be named Bombay Cloth House, but it does not mean that the village is in Bombay. Similarly, there is no relation of the *Saraswati* veena with the Goddess Saraswati.

According to Bharat in *Natya Shastra*, "Narada's veena was named Mehti veena. It had twenty-one strings and was played with finger nail. Another veena named Vipanchi was made by Rishi Swati and it had nine strings."

Modifications of Old Veenas

The development or modification of the *Tri-tantri* veena started in the thirteenth or fourteenth centuries. In his book *Ain-i-Akbari*, written in about 1598, Abul Faz-i-allami wrote, "The Yantra or Jantar is formed of a hollow neck of wood, a yard in length, with two gourds at each end. It has sixteen frets, five steel wires. The low and high notes and their variations are produced by the disposition of the frets."

Tat vadhyas, or stringed instruments, have gone through several ages—the Vedic period, the ancient period, the middle ages, and the modern period.

1. Vedic period—There was only one string for every *swara* and one hollow gourd was fitted on the left side of the pipe or *daand*. It was touched or plucked with the index fingernail.
2. Ancient period—A plectrum or bow was used to produce a resonant sound. Sometimes a long stick called *shalaka* was used to produce *swaras* on the veena.
3. Middle age—In the tenth century, the frets were attached to the fingerboard for showing the *swar-sthan* or pitch of *swaras*. The frets were called *sundaries* or *sarikaas*. The main string was on the inside of the fingerboard, and the gourd was on the left side and was kept on the shoulder of the player. In this period, the tenth century, the *Tri-tantri* veena was modified with frets attached to the fingerboard, and the player could produce four to five *swaras* on one string, whereas it was difficult for the veena *vaadak* to reach so many *swaras* on an *Ek-tantri* or a previous form of the *Tri-tantri* veena.
4. Modern period—The last, but not the least, changes started in the thirteenth century as far as the string instruments are concerned. All the stringed instruments such as the sitar, the *sur-bahar*, the *vichitra* veena, the sarod, the *sarangi*, the *Israj*, and the *dilruba* now have the same style of putting the frets on the fingerboard.

The main strings are on the outside and are plucked with a plectrum worn on the index finger of the right hand. The frets are called "*Pardas*."

Historical Background of Stringed Instruments

I, as a curious inquirer, explored the details of the history of world instruments to learn if the sitar is of Indian origin or from a different country.

I consulted many books, such as *The Universal History of Music* and *Instruments of the World,* by Raja Sir S. M. Tagore, and *Vishva Sangeet Ka Itihas,* by Amal Dash Sharma. I visited Canada and the United States, where I gathered material. I went to Saskatoon University and Calgary University in Canada and the State Library in New York, where I consulted many books on the history of stringed instruments of the world and those that are prevalent in other countries. I took pictures of the instruments that are preserved in the department of music in Saskatoon University.

Here are the results of my survey:
1. Thailand—An instrument named *Tur-kay* is popular there. It has three silken threads as strings, and it has frets. This instrument is played with a plectrum and is similar to the veena's shape.
2. Burma—The *Saung* or *Soum* is a boat-type instrument with thirteen silken strings and is played with a plectrum. Another instrument that is common in Burma is the *Thro*. This is also like the Indian veena.
3. Russia—The lyre is very popular in Russia. It is made of tortoise skin with seven strings attached, and then it is played with a plectrum.
4. Greece—Pythagoras agreed that the lyre with seven strings, which is common in Greece, became popular in the medieval period with the name of the sitar, but no evidence is available as to its origin.
5. China—The Indian lute (veena) was very famous in the period between 2855 and 2735 BC, during the time of the mythical sage and emperor Fu-Hsi.
6. Arabs—Raja Sir S. M. Tagore wrote in his *Universal History of Music*: "There are two types of Rabab prevalent in Arab, one is Rabab-a-shaer and the other is Rabab-esh moganny.

    The *Rabab* prevalent in Java and Sumatra is a modification of Indian *Ek-tara* and has two strings. The *Rabab* is only a modification of the veena of the Hindus, the only difference being in body of the instrument."

    Actually, the *Rabab* is a Muslim instrument with a wide, shallow *bown,* made of wood, covered with parchment. It is something like a shortened sitar, but has no frets. The *Ek-tara* has also one open string and no frets. So, one thing common in one country is copied by musicians in another. This is an obvious fact.
7. Japan—Amal Kumar Dash Sharma wrote in *Vishwa Sangeet Ka Itihas*: "There are so many stringed instruments prevalent in Japan (one string to 13 stringed). The one stringed instrument is called Summa-koto, and 13 stringed instrument is named Lono-Koto. Another instrument prevalent in ancient period in Japan was

Biwa, which was made of sandal wood with beautiful carvings and had five strings. In ancient period, the scale was only of five swaras, but now they have seven swaras like Indian music."

8. Sri Lanka—Amal Kumar Dash Sharma also writes of an instrument in Sri Lanka called the *Venrah* or *Venah*, which has two strings. It has a gourd of coconut and a long fingerboard on which two strings are fitted with pegs. This instrument is played with a bow.

9. Persia—From the same source, we learn of the *Qanun*, which had seventy-two strings, was of Persian origin, and had the shape of the Indian sitar. Another instrument in Persia was the *Taus* or *Mayuri*, a peacock fiddle, which was also similar to the sitar. It took its name from the peacock-like resonator.

10. Italy— A two-stringed *Do-tara* instrument named *calascione* is famous and is also played with a plectrum.

11. Palestine—A veena-type harp, the ten-stringed *Acor*, and a dulcimer like the *Ek-tara* are very popular.

12. Ireland—Michael Conran wrote in his book *National Music of Ireland*, 1846: "A photograph of veena-type harp is lying in the church of Kilkenny city, which seems just like veena and the harp is kept in the player's lap."

13. Russia—The two-stringed balalaika, the five-stringed *Guzali*, the veena-type *Rilke*, and the three-stringed *Torban* are very common.

14. North America—An Intuit (Eskimo) tribe living on the northwest border of Canada believes that an instrument like the two-stringed *Vac-a-tat* and *kush-tar-kar* were given to them by an Indian tribe, according to Dr. David Kaplin in Saskatoon, Canada, who has a vast understanding of world instruments.
    When the civilizations vanish and are replaced by a new one, old artifacts disappear.

15. Germany—A harp-type instrument named the zither was common. It had three strings and was played with fingernails. This name is also the synonym of the sitar but because no written evidence is available, we can't say that the sitar is the same instrument which was once the zither.

16. Bible—The Bible mentions a *Kinnor*, which is a beggar's instrument these days. It might have some connection with Indian *Kinnari* veena, which we find in old sculptures and paintings.

So, as the time passes, civilizations change, the art and culture possessed by one civilization is taken over by another civilization or dynasty. The intermingling of different cultures then gives birth to a new culture. The Indian sitar has also come a long way.

In Greece, it is believed that when the Greeks fought on the northern sector of their own country in sixteenth century, they brought with them slaves, who had with them instruments called *Cithesses* instead of weapons. This instrument was also called *Guzali* in their Salabh language.

The *Salaabh sangeet* was popular in the whole Europe in tenth century.

The *Cithess* or *Guzali* had three strings. So we see, though there was vast distance between places, the Russian *Guzali* was popular in Greece.

H. A. Popley writes in his book, *The Music Of India*: "There is a beautiful sitar in *Gandharva Mahavidhalaya* Bombay, which has an ostrich egg for the bowl, beautifully mounted with gold. Some sitars have peacock shaped heads and are called peacock sitars."

Conclusion

After studying the history of musical instruments of the world, I reached the conclusion that the *Ek-tara* or *Ek-tantri* veena was the basic instrument. It then made a long journey, during which it underwent many modifications in shape, size, and techniques, by many musicians in different places in different times.

The changes were:

1. The basic instrument, the *Ek-tantri* veena, had only one string.
2. The second string added to the *Ek-tara* or *Ek-tantri* veena became the *Do-tara*.
3. It received another modification with the addition of one more string and became the *Tri-tantri* veena.
4. Twelve frets were added to the fingerboard, and it was named the *kinnari* veena.
5. When this instrument was decorated with nineteen frets, it was called the *Dilruba*.

6. The Persians added a new modification when they removed the frets but kept the four strings as were on the *Tambur*, and they called the result the *Rabab*.
7. It received another alteration and was called *Taus* or *Mayuri* or Peacock Fiddle.

The *Ek-tantri* veena had a fingerboard, a gourd, and the string kept tight by one peg. Most of the early Indian musical instruments that were described in old Sanskrit treatises, paintings, and sculptures, such as those of Ajanta, prove this even more conclusively.

Some details are given, which at first sight seem to be unnecessary but throw much light upon several questions.

Alain Danielow wrote in his book, *Introduction to the Study of Musical Scales*:

> "Musical instruments were also introduced into Chinese music from India, such as Tumbu veena or Tanpura, which the Chinese call Tan-pu-la, and the Taba or Arabic drum which became Ta-pu-laeh. Persian instruments were also introduced such as sitar which the Chinese call Sa-tho-eul and the Sarangi which is called as Sa-long-tri etc. in Chinese language."

The Persian sitar with three strings is in use today also, in Hyderabad and Jaipur. Since the time of the Mohammedan invasion in the tenth century (about a thousand years ago), some Arabian and Persian instruments have been adopted in India, but their use is confined mostly to Muslim musicians only.

CHAPTER 3

Origin of the Sitar

An Analytical Study of the Origin of the Sitar

The sitar is the most popular instrument in India today. There are various theories and opinions about the origin of sitar. We find some references in the Indian history about this instrument in the thirteenth century and then in the eighteenth century. I have already discussed in detail the stringed instruments of the Vedic and ancient periods, so we know about the veenas prevalent in those times. It is a hard fact that the *Tri-tantri* veena is the base of the sitar, but there have been changes to the arrangement of strings, the name, the tuning, and the plucking technique of the medieval veena, and one gourd has been added to make the south Indian veena. The sitar, on the contrary, has the nucleus of modern strings and tuning. It is an accepted fact that the sitar is a descendant of the veena that was common in India during the tenth century, but who was the inventor of the sitar?

There are several versions of the origin of the sitar:

- The sitar was an Iranian/Persian instrument.
- Ameer Khusro invented the *Sehtaar*, which became the sitar.
- The ancient *Tri-tantri* veena was given a new name—*Seh-taar*—by Ameer Khusro. In his own Persian language, "*Tri-tantri*" became "*Seh-taar.*"

The renowned Indian musician Naushaad Sahib said in a TV interview on November 19, 1992, that Ameer Khusro brought the *"Seh-taar"* from Iran and set three more strings on this instrument. The Muslims put on one more string, which was called *chikari*.

- According to Abul Fazal in *Aine-Akbari*, Ameer Khusro invented *"Ta-taar."*
- Pt. Ravi Shankar ji gives evidence of the invention of the sitar by Ameer Khusro in his book *My Music, My Life*.
- Mubarak Hussain Khan writes in his book, *Music and Its Study*: "Ameer Khusro was the inventor of the string instrument 'sitar.' 'Seh' means three, and taar means strings, and hence the name."
- The sitar is a modification of the *kinnari* or *Tri-tantri* or *Sapat-tantri* veena.
- According to Pt. Omkar Nath Thakur, writing in *Bhartiya Sangeet*, "In *Maharashtra*, the *'Sattar'* was a very popular instrument of seven strings. Then, this instrument took the name of *'Satar'* and people eventually started calling it by the name of sitar."
- According to Raja Sir S. M. Tagore in his book, *Yantra Kshetra Deepika*: "The sitar is the changed form of the Nibadh Tambur. It had five to six strings." Tagore also wrote that "The ancient *Tri-tantri* veena was given a new name by Ameer Khustro, in Persian language, as 'Seh-taar.'"

Another opinion by Dr. Indrani Chakarvarty in her book, *Swara aur Vadhyon Ka Yogdaan*: "Jantra had five strings and sixteen frets, so sitar is originated from this instrument."

An analytical study is needed to make out a solution to the origin of the sitar.

During the eleventh and twelfth centuries, Persian became the official language of the whole Indian Empire. The double-reed *Shehnai Suran* was adopted by Hindus as well as by the Muslims. The *Shehnai* reached the South but under a new name—*Nagaswaram*.

However, when Khusro Malik was succeeded by Mohammed Gauri in the year 1186, he took over the regime of Lahore in his own hands. Khusro Malik had been a musician, but he was enslaved by Mohammed Gauri, and so there is no literature to be found written by Khusro Malik.

In the time of Alaudin Khilji (AD 1296 to AD 1316), Ameer Khusro was a great Persian poet and musician. He mixed Persian, Arabic, and Turkish styles of music with the inherited music of the subcontinent. He is known for the vital role played in the enrichment of the music of that period. Through his efforts, music rose to the heights of popularity. He was the sole important musician of that period, and, in the thirteenth century, we find no other musician's name in Indian history such as his who advanced instrumental music. He remained unrivaled for centuries.

Shri Bhagwat Sharan Sharma wrote in 1958 in *Sitar Malika*, "Though we find about sixty names of veenas in old treatises, but when we come across the thirteenth century's music, we find the name of Ameer Khusro, who is said to be the inventor of sitar."

As the three-stringed veena existed, he can't be *the* inventor, but it is a hard fact, that, as a Persian, he renamed the *Tri-tantri* veena as *Seh-taar* in his own language, which means three-stringed instrument.

It is very important to note four prominent names that are similar to each other and may be confused:

1. Khusro Malik—AD 1186
2. Ameer Khusro—AD 1246–AD 1316
3. Meer Khusro—AD 1657–AD 1707
4. Khusro Khan—AD 1670–AD 1748

    1. Khusro Malik—In the year 1186, he was the ruler of Lahore but was succeeded by Mohammed Gauri. Khusro Malik was a lover of music, but we find nothing written by him on music or by any other writers about him as a musician, so he can't be the inventor of sitar.

    2. Ameer Khusro—Ameer Khusro's father, Mohammed Shaifudin, came to India from Khorasan, a city in Faras (Persia). Ameer Khusro was born in Uttar Pradesh in Patiali village, in the Etta District. From the very beginning of his childhood, he was musically talented, and he became a great musician and poet of that period. He joined the court of the king of Kaikubad, where he remained from 1287 to 1290. Then, he came to the court of King Jalaludin Khilji, where he received the title of Ameer, though his actual name was Abul Hasan. In 1296, he received the title of Khusru-e-shairan. In

one of his famous books, *Dawalrani Khijri*, Ameer Khusro has described about one Utsav, which was held at the marriage of Alaudin Khilji's son.

"Another musician Gopal Nayak was also present. He was an expert in singing Rag Kadam, a kind of long song, containing 32 ragas and so many talas."

In 1316, Ameer Khusro joined the court of Kutbuddin Khilji, where he remained until 1320. He first became a musician in the court of Gayasudin Tughlak, and then moved to Muhammad Tughlak's court in 1325. Ameer Khusro had previously met Gopal Nayak, who was a court singer in North India's Devgiri Riyasat, whose king was Ram-Chander. So Gopal Nayak was brought to the court of Delhi where the two musicians made great efforts together to raise the standards of music.

According to the Ministry of Information and Broadcasting in Delhi's *Facts about India*, published in 1960: "Ameer Khusro gave a new name to the Tri tantric veena as 'Seh taar' and added three more strings to the instrument. He invented new Ragas —Sarparda, Sazgiri, Yaman, Raat Ki Pooriya, Poorvi, Todi, Mazeer etc."

3. Meer Khusro—Meer Khusro's name appears in Indian history in Aurangzeb's time, 1657–1707, but we find none of his works on music or musical instrument. Music declined in Aurangzeb's time, as he did not like music. He buried many musical instruments as history tells us, but kept some of them and some musicians for the recreation at one or the other occasion.

It is wrong to connect this name with the invention of the sitar, because we don't find his name in the list of the musicians of that period who were Khushaal Khan, Visram Khan, Hayyat Khan, Sarasnain Khan, Sukhisen Kalawant, and Kripa.

4. Khusro Khan—In the period of Muhammad Shah Rangeley, 1670–1748, the name of Nemat Khan or Sadarang was famous in the history of Indian music, and his works are remembered still. He was a great singer of his time. His younger brother, Khusro Khan, also came to prominence

along with his brother, and the rumor spread that he had invented a new instrument named the sitar, but, in fact, it already existed.

H. A. Popley wrote in his *Music of India,* "History tells us about the invention of Rabab and Surbahar by Tansen on the basis of Sehtaar or sitar and Veena." The *Sehtaar,* which had originated in the thirteenth century, had taken its name as the sitar in the due course of time.

Though the *Tambur, Rabab,* and *Sarangi* were common in those days, the sitar could not become popular with the vocalists because vocal music was at its heights.

Acharya Brahaspati has given many names of the instrumentalists and singers, including Hasan Khan's name in connection with *"Sitar Baaj,"* which he used in his *"Been."* It clarifies that the sitar already existed in the thirteenth century. Some persons—if only a few—knew how to play it, so it is wrong to say that Kusro Khan invented the sitar.

Abul Fazal wrote in his book *Aine-Akbari*: "Ameer Khusro invented the *'Ta-taar.'"* It must be a printing mistake because wherever Ameer Khusro's contributions are discussed in other references, we find only the word *'Sehtaar,'* so it might be *'Sehtaar.'*

I interviewed Shujjat Husain Khan on Feburary 11, 1993, in the Rose Garden, Kala Bhawan, Sector 16, Chandigarh, where he had come to give a sitar recital. He said: "I never went into the theory part, nor did I read much about the origin of the sitar. But Ameer Khusro is said to be the inventor of sitar."

In the magazine, *Sangeet,* a Sangeet Karyalya Hathras publication, 1978: "In Turkey and Iranian literature, we find the name of Sehtaar."

The period of almost two hundred years following Ameer Khusro is considered to be the dark period in northern India's history. Wars were raged continuously, art and cultural progress came to a standstill. There was devastation all over, which gave a set back to music and musicians of that period. Though in Akbar's time (sixteenth century) music flourished. Tansen, Baiju Bawra, and Swami Haridas were great musicians of that period.

Hathras Publications' *Sangeet Karyalya* of 1978 said: "Tansen invented Rabab on the basis of 'Seh taar' and veena." This evidence shows the presence of the modern sitar in the name of "Seh tar."

Here are the words of the great sitar maestro of international fame, Pt. Ravi Shankar ji, who has given some of the details of the sitar in his book, *My Music, My Life*:

> "Shortly after the time of Sharangdev, there lived an extraordinary inventor and genius, Ameer Khusro, who was not only an unrivaled scholar and lover of music and skilled musician but also a poet and statesman. He was of Persian lineage, but was born and brought up in India. He acquired his musical fame at the court of Sultan Alaudin Khilji, a Pathan ruler of Delhi, where he was a celebrated singer. Because of his musical talents and immense imitative powers, he was called "Shrutidar," a name given to one who can reproduce any sound, musical or nonmusical, even if he had heard it only once.
>
> It is not unnatural that since he had such prominent positions, the historians of that time gave him the credit for many things that he really did not bring about. He is nonetheless responsible for a number of modifications of musical instruments and in particular sitar for creating some ragas that are heard today and for developing and popularizing some well-known styles of singing.
>
> Many scholars believe that sitar was in existence long before Ameer Khusro's time, in diverse shapes, in different regions of India. It was variously called *Tri-tantri* veena (Sanskrit meaning 'three stringed'), Chitra veena (seven stringed) or Parivadini. But it is an unavoidable fact that Ameer Khusro did make certain alterations and gave a new name 'Seh-taar' (Persian for 'three stringed')."

Innovations in Strings and Frets

The order of the strings was reversed giving the instrument the present-day, universal arrangement of the strings. Another ancient stringed instrument, the *Been*, still has its strings in the old 'inside out' order; that is, the main playing string is on the inside and the bass strings are on the outside part of the instrument.

Pt.Ravi Shankar ji wrote in his book, *My Music My Life* "Another improvement that Ameer Khusro brought to the sitar was to make the frets moveable (frets are the metal or brass strips that go across the fingerboard of the instrument).

On the older instruments, such as the veena, the frets were fixed with wax and hence could not be moved. Ameer Khusro attached silken string or thin gut to the frets and tied them at the back of the sitar's neck, so that the player could move the frets up and down. According to this method, the fingerboard was divided into the seven-note octave after eliminating some frets, and they could be moved up or down for the use of half or whole tones."

Saifudin Fakeerullah, in his *Rag Darpan* of 1663, reported that "Ameer Khusro made the following ragas: *Muwakif, Ush-Shak, Sarparda, Sajgiri, Ba-Karaj, Mazeer, Gaman, Fargaan, Sanam Zeelaf, Farodast, Yemni, Aiman* and *Basant*. He made an instrument called 'Seh-taar' with three strings."

To make it clearer that Ameer Khusro made great contributions to music and musical instruments, one has to go into the depth of history of the middle age—those of the early thirteenth century. The Devgiri Dynasty came to an end in southern India because of the attack by the Yawans on India, and this had a bad effect on the music of India. This was the time when the instruments and ragas of Persia came to India. Delhi was under Sultan Alaudin Khilji's rule from 1216 to 1296, and music flourished in his time like a stream, because in his court there was a great musician and court singer named Abul Hassan, who with his talents in music pleased the sultan and was conferred the title of *Ameer* and *Khusro-a-shairan*. It is said that he was the first Turk who mixed the Persian and Indian ragas and brought innovation to the music.

The third version of how "Sattar" became "sitar" is totally wrong, as there is no reference of this, except that Pt. Omkar Nath said it.

Views of the Famous Authors

Here are some of the opinions of authors who have given their own ideas about the origin of the sitar:

1. Dev Vrat Cahudnary, in *The Sitar and Its Techniques*: "Tri tantri veena, when modified became 'Jantar' and with further changes it took the name of sitar."

2. Dr. Indrani Chakarvarty, in *Swara Aur Vadhyon Ka Yogdaan*: "Jantar of Rajasthan, which was prevalent in middle age, was a modification of Kinnari veena, so Jantar or Kinnari veena can be referred to as the Mother of Sitar, because Tri tantri veena and Jantar had the frets."

3. *Facts about India,* published by the Ministry of Information and Broadcasting: "Sitar, a stringed instrument with its feminine grace, is believed to have been devised by Ameer Khusro in the 14th century."

4. Vishambar Nath Bhatt, in *Sitar Shiksha* (fifth edition): "Sitar was invented by Ameer Khusro as Veena was difficult to learn, so he modified the *Tri-tantri* veena, which had *Baaj* ka taar, Shadaj and Pancham string."

5. Panna Lal Madan, in *Bhartiya Sangeet Aur Uska Vikas*: "Alaudin Khilji's minister Ameer Khusro introduced an instrument, which he named 'Seh-taar.'"

6. Shripad Vandopadhya, in *Sitar Marg*: "Hazrat Ameer Khusro popularized *Tri-tantri* veena as 'Seh-taar' or Alah-Baja, means, three-stringed instrument."

7. Arvind Parikh, in a 1968 essay in *Sangeet*: "Abul Hassan, who is known as Ameer Khusro, invented this instrument 'Seh-taar' on the basis of Veena."

8. Shanti Govardhan, in *Sangeet Shastar Darpan*: "In fourteenth century, Ameer Khusro invented 'Seh-taar' on the basis of Veena and Tanpura. He gave the name 'Seh-taar' which means three strings. Jalaludin gave the honor of 'Ameer' to Abul Hasan because he was a great musician and inventor of 'Seh-taar.' Alaudin Khilji and Tughlak also gave this 'Upadhi' to him because he invented 'Seh-taar'."

From the above survey, it seems most likely that the sitar was in fact originally a three-stringed instrument, such as the *Tri-tantri* instrument, that was given the name of *"Seh-taar,"* which became "sitar" with the passage of time.

Swaras of the Vedic, Ancient, and Modern Periods (Historical Survey)

When we discuss the instrument, we must know about the *swaras* it produces, so the origin of its *swaras* is a point of historical survey. Which *swaras* were used in the Vedic period in music, both vocal and played on the veena?

There were three categories of *swaras* in the Vedic period:

1. *Udata* — *Ni   Ga*
2. *Anudata* — *Re   Dha*
3. *Swarit* — *Sa   Ma   Pa*

The scale was divided into two tetra chords as follows:

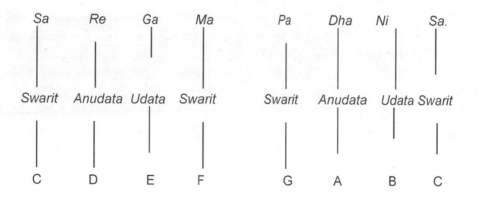

Purvanga (lower)				*Uttarang* (upper)			
Sa	Re	Ga	Ma	Pa	Dha	Ni	Sa.
Swarit	Anudata	Udata	Swarit	Swarit	Anudata	Udata	Swarit
C	D	E	F	G	A	B	C

Sam-ved Period—The seven notes were:

1. *Prathma* — *Ma* — First
2. *Dvitiya* — *Ge* — Second
3. *Tritiya* — *Ra* — Third
4. *Chaturatha* — *Sa* — Fourth

5.	*Pancham*	—	*Pa*	—	Fifth
6.	*Atiswara*	—	*Ni*	—	Extreme note
7.	*Krushtha*	—	*Dha*	—	Pulled, dragged

These *swaras* were set on sitar according to the *Gram*, which means a family and its members. There were three grams:

1. Shadaj gram
2. Madhayam gram
3. Gandhaar gram

Sharangdev in *Sangeet Ratnakar* wrote: "Chatushchatushchaiv Shadaj Madhyam Panchma Dvai Dvai Nishaad Gandharou, Tristro Rishabh Dhaiwato."

Shadaj, Madhyam and Pancham notes have 4 shruties each.

Nishaad and Gandhar have 2 shruties each.

Rishabh and Dhaivat have 3 shruties each.

Sa *swara* was considered to be *Achal* swara.

Ancient Period—The octave was divided into twenty-two intervals called "*shruties.*"

Middle Age and Modern Age—The Hindu octave was divided into twenty-two semitones.

The twenty-two shruties were:

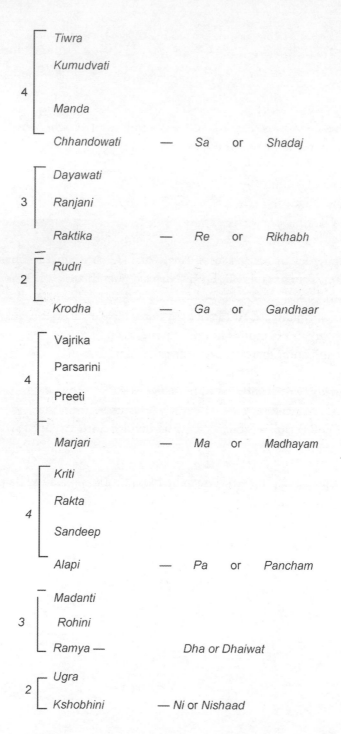

4
- *Tiwra*
- *Kumudvati*
- *Manda*
- *Chhandowati* — Sa or Shadaj

3
- *Dayawati*
- *Ranjani*
- *Raktika* — Re or Rikhabh

2
- *Rudri*
- *Krodha* — Ga or Gandhaar

4
- Vajrika
- Parsarini
- Preeti
- *Marjari* — Ma or Madhayam

4
- *Kriti*
- *Rakta*
- *Sandeep*
- *Alapi* — Pa or Pancham

3
- *Madanti*
- *Rohini*
- *Ramya* — Dha or Dhaiwat

2
- *Ugra*
- *Kshobhini* — Ni or Nishaad

1. The scale that begins with *Sa* is called *Shadaj gram.*
2. The scale that begins with *Ga* is known as *Gandhaar gram.*
3. The scale that starts from *Ma* is called as *Madhyam gram.*

The difference of *shruties* has already been shown above in the three *grams.* Ancient musicians, as well as the musicians of today, agreed on this point. These *shruties* are also known by the same names today.

To study and understand all these different intervals and to accustom the ear to them, it is necessary to have an instrument that allows their accurate execution. The simplest is, of course, a stringed instrument of sufficient dimensions, an Indian sitar for example, with moveable frets and with the exact placement of *shruties* marked on the side on which the frets move.

To mark these places, the tension of the *swaras* is kept in mind, and then a mark is made on the wood, so that the fret may easily be returned whenever the same note is desired. This is to be done with all the *swaras* of the scale. The whole length of the instrument is marked. By changing the place of the fret, the correct tuning for each mode is obtained.

All the twenty-two divisions can't be utilized simultaneously in a mode or in any melodic or harmonic combination. At the most, twelve, and at the least, five notes are used—the normal number being seven.

C. R. Day wrote in *The Music and Musical Instruments of Southern India and the Deccan*:

> "The science of the sound is the chemistry of the universe. If the *shruties* and frets are set right, the sound of the notes will be accurate and accuracy of *swaras* has such a great power to influence the animate and inanimate things. From among these 22 *shruties*, we have seven Shudh *swaras*, (natural notes), four Komal *swaras* (flat notes), one is Tiwra *swara*, (sharp note). In the arrangement of the *shruties*, modern usage is diametrically opposite to the classical one, the later placing them before the note to which they respectively belong, while the former gives their position after the notes. It is difficult to determine when or by whom the alteration was effected. The arrangement of the frets of veena and other stringed instruments accord with the modern acceptation of the principle. In the classical treatise, the disposition of the notes is reversed in the case of stringed instruments and out of this reversed arrangement

perhaps, the modern theory about the arrangement of the position of the *shruties* has been worked out."

Changing Forms of the Sitar, Thirteenth to Sixteenth Century

Change is the inherent nature of the world, and change and development are inevitable in every phenomenon. Change is also a part and parcel of human society. So we find new and novel forms and types from time to time. The sitar has also come a long way. The thirteenth and fourteenth century's examples make it clear that the *Seh-taar* had three strings. But when Ameer Khusro added three more strings to this instrument and the Muslims added one *chikari* string, it became a seven-stringed instrument.

As Vasant wrote in *Sangeet Visharad*: "In the sixteenth century, Imratsen and Nihalsen put an extra gourd on the back of the daand of sitar which lengthened the 'Aass' of the string, which helped in solo *vaadan* of sitar."

In the beginning it had eleven sympathetic strings (*Tarabs*) and seven main strings. Here is the detailed description of Pt. Ravi Shankar ji's sitar in *My Music, My Life*:

"Strings	Tuning	Material	Gauge used
1. *Baaj ki taar*	.M	High carbon musical steel wire	30
2. *Jore ki taar*	.S	Bronze	27
3. *Jore ki taar*	.S		27
4. *Mandra*	.p	Bronze	21
5. *Ati Mandra*	.P	High carbon steel	32
6. *Madhaya*	Sa	This string can be left off entirely to facilitate playing	33
7. *Chikari*	Sa.	High carbon	34"

"1. *Baaj* String—This is the main string on which *swaras* are produced when we press on it with the index finger of our left hand. In the thirteenth and fourteenth centuries, it was called the *Madhyam* string or *Nayaki* string. Today, this word has almost been discarded, and the first string is called *Baaj Ka Taar*. This string is tuned as *Madhayam* of *Mandra Saptak*.

2. and 3. *Jore ka taar*—Inside the *Baaj ka Taar*, there are two strings tuned into *shadaj* of *Mandra Saptak*.

4. The fourth string is tuned into *pancham* of *Mandra Saptak*.

5. This is tuned into *ati mandra Pancham* of *Mandra Saptak*.

6. The next (sixth) string is tuned into shadaj of *Madhya Saptak*.

7. Then comes the seventh string. It is called *chikari* or *papaya* string. It is tuned into *shadaj* of *Taar-Saptak*. In *alaap* or *jhala*, this string brings beauty and charm whenever the player wants to have a little pause. He makes a continuity of the raga with this string by striking it in rhythm. It helps to enrich the beauty and sweetness in sitar *vaadan*," according to Vasant, in his book, Sangeet Visharad.

Sixteenth to nineteenth centuries—

Dev Vrat Cahaudray has written in his book, *Sitar and Its Techniques*:
"Though the technique of tuning the instrument remains the same today, as it was done in the beginning, but the curious musician always makes the changes. The first tarb tuned to Madhya Shadaj, second to Mandra Nishaad and third again to Madhya Shadaj. Then all the remaining *tarabs* were tuned according to the *swaras* of the raga to be played. If these strings are tuned accurately then these strings make a resonant sound while the upper bass strings are played."

In Abul Fazal's time, the Jantar had existed with fine strings and sixteen frets.

Twentieth century—

Sharmistha Sen has written in *String Instruments of North India*: "Until the year 1950, Kachchapi veena was played by the artists which had a flattened gourd and it had tarab strings also. The name was Kachchapi because it had a shape of Kachhua. It had 16 frets and had seven upper strings."

In the middle of twentieth century, the sitar had adopted its shape with a round gourd, nineteen frets, seven upper strings, and eleven *tarabs*.

However, great artists innovate in their art. Pt. Ravi Shankar ji of Senia *Gharana* has written in *My Music, My Life* of how he has kept only five strings in his sitar:

"1. *Baaj* ki Taar
2. Jore ki Taar
3. Mandra Pancham
4. Kharaj ki Taar
5. Chikari or Papeeha."

The sitar has the highest place in all the stringed instruments. The frets and strings can be different in every musician's sitar and arranged as they want. The player sets his sitar according to his convenience

Different Types of Sitars

There are basically two types of sitars:

*   Simple sitar
*   *Tarafdar* sitar

Simple sitar—It has seven strings and no *tarabs*. It is suited for beginners because it is small in form and size. It has a gourd with a two-foot long fingerboard. A bridge is placed on the gourd and then the strings are set on the fingerboard and tied with the pegs fitted on the inner side and upper side of the fingerboard.

Tarafdar sitar—The second type of sitar has seven strings and eleven sympathetic *tarabs* placed beneath the upper strings. Though the sympathetic strings are never played, they give a continuous humming (*Jhankaar*) as the upper strings are played. Sometimes the artist just touches them with the *mizraab* in such a way that they produce very sweet sounds. The length of the sitar is four and a half feet. Its fingerboard is thirty-four inches long and is three inches wide. The frets are tied on the fingerboard with the pegs. The fingerboard is made of *Sheesham* wood, *Tanu* wood, or Burma teak wood. The back side of the fingerboard is round in shape with a leveled wood piece fitted on it, in which the spring holes are positioned to adjust *tarabs* and the frets are fitted on it.

Besides these two types of sitars, we find two other sitars designated in accordance with their frets:

- *Chal Thaat ki* sitar
- *Achal Thaat ki* sitar

1. *Chal Thaat ki* sitar—Until 1930, these sitars had sixteen frets:

.M	.P	.Dha	Dha	.Ni	Sa	Re	Ga
Ma	Ma/	Pa	Dha	Ni	Sa.	Re.	Ga.

There are many ragas in which a particular *swara* is used in *Aroh* but is not used in *Avroh*, so to produce the needed *swara* by pulling the string every time is a tough job, when played at high speed. For example, in raga *Sarang, Des* and Khamaj, *Ni Shudh* is used in their *Aroh* and *komal Ni* in *Avrohan*. In the sixteen-fretted sitar, there was only one *Ni*, hence the problem. To avoid this obstacle, the musicians put on three more frets. With this, the number of frets became nineteen and the following *swaras* were derived from these frets:

.Ma	.Pa	.Dha	.Dha	.Ni	.Ni	Sa	Re	G	G
Ma	Ma/	Pa	Dha	Ni	Ni	Sa.	Re.	G.	

Re, Dha komal is produced by raising *shudh Re* and *Dha*.

Some people attach one more fret for *taar saptak's Ma Swara,* so that they can reach up to full *taar saptak* or upper octave.

Until 1950 or so, only *baaj ka taar* was used in the sitars for playing purposes, while the others were just touched to produce resonant sound. But with the new experiments, after getting *mandra Ma* from *baaj ka taar,* we get *mandra Ga, Re Sa* from *Jore ki taar.* For *ati mandra Ni Dha Pa,* we play the *Ati mandra Pancham* string, and in the end for *Ati mandra Ma Ga Re Sa,* we play the *Ati mandra shadaj* string.

2. *Achal Thaat* Ki sitar—In this sitar, there are twenty-four frets:

.Ma .Pa .<u>Dha</u> . Dha .<u>Ni</u> .Ni Sa Re <u>Re</u> <u>Ga</u> Ga Ma

Ma/ Pa <u>Dha</u> Dha <u>Ni</u> Ni Sa. <u>Re.</u> Re. <u>Ga.</u> Ga. Ma.

This type of sitar has the capacity to play all the *swaras* of the ragas without moving the frets.

This sitar is not in much use today, because the same distance of the *swaras* creates confusion in the mind of the sitar player about *swaras.* Above all, sometimes that *swara* is touched which is *Varjit* in the raga, so the modern musician does not prefer this sitar. The small distance in frets is a hindrance for the fingers also.

So, we see that even though there have been so many changes in the frets, *tarabs,* and strings, the sitar has reached the heights of popularity and respect in the world of music. The modern sitar has developed after many modifications in shape, size, and techniques. The nineteen-fretted sitars have the capacity to play three *saptaks* or scales, which can cover all the nine rasas or *bhavas* described in Indian culture.

The Structural Forms of the Sitar

The sitar has existed in various shapes and sizes in the past, as has been explained in the preceding sections. Different numbers of frets and strings were in use simultaneously. Although this situation still persists, the sitar used for concerts and for learners has become fairly standardized. An artist can customize his sitar to some extent to suit his particular style of playing or he can adjust the timbre to his taste, but these are usually minor adjustments, such as changing the curvature of the bridge. The instrument is specifically termed as *Chal Thaat Tarafdaar* sitar, because it incorporates a set of sympathetically resonating wires (*tarafs*) under the frets and because the frets need to be repositioned for certain scale types.

Here are the details of a sitar's construction and the functional use:

(a) **Gourd**—The belly is made of Jack or some other resonant wood, such as *tumba*. The gourd is emptied from inside so that the sound gives the proper effect when the strings are pressed. The gourd is the main resonating chamber of the instrument.

(b) *Tabli*—This is the soundboard. It is fourteen inches wide. The thinness of the *tabli* is important, because it is the part where the bridge or *Jawari* is placed; the curve is a work of art. It is slightly convex in shape in order to make it more resilient. Its thinness provides more resonance, but it should be thick enough to withstand the pressure of the strings.

(c) *Gulu*—When the gourd and *tabli* are fixed, the *Gulu* is the point where these two are to be joined together. The main structural function of the *Gulu* is to provide a strong base through which the *Daand* may be indirectly joined to the gourd resonator.

(d) *Langot* or *Longorus* or **Keel**—This is a small triangular piece of deer horn or a nail that works as an anchor to which all the strings are attached. It is set on the lower portion of the *tumba*, from which all the wires go to their destinations.

(e) *Daand*—This pipe is thirty-four inches long and three inches wide. It is the neck of the instrument. Burmese teak wood is best for making a *daand*, but some sitar makers use *sheesham* or *Tanu* wood also. The back side of the *daand* is round in shape, to which a leveled wood piece is fitted. Then, the string holes are done on the upper part of the fingerboard to adjust *tarabs* and frets fitted on it.

(f) *Jawari* or *Ghurach*—This is the bridge of the sitar, a flat plate of ivory, over which the seven playing strings pass. The distance between *longorus* and *ghurach* is four inches. The *ghurach* is three inches long and one inch wide. The upper portion of the *ghurach* is known as the *Jawari*. The top part is fashioned from an antelope horn; the bottom from tun wood. In order to produce an even, rich sound, the *Jawari* must be filed to a precise curvature. The filing technique is a highly specialized craft and there are only a few sitar makers in India who can produce a good *Jawari*. Rikhi Ram was the most renowned in this art work.

(g) **Small bridge**—This is also a small piece of antelope horn made into a one and a half by one inch bridge. The eleven *tarabs* are put on it. From the *longot* they pass through the *daand* holes.

(h) ***Ati* or *Pacisa***—The *Ati* is located seven and a half inches from the end of the *daand* and is three-quarters of an inch high. This is a flat piece that supports the five wires. Its main function is to keep the strings at the level of the bridge. Five small cuts are made in the ivory piece, so that the strings don't slip and remain in one place.

(i) ***Taargahan***—The *Taargahan* is fitted at a place called *Meru*, which is fashioned in the same shape as the *Ati*. Its width corresponds to the fingerboard. There are five main holes in it, through which the wires pass and then are tied to the pegs. The lower position of the holes in the *Taar gahan* ensures that the wires fit securely into the slots of the Taar gahan.

(j) ***Darh***—These are two small posts made of antelope horn that is inserted ventrally into the *daand* on the right side of the instrument. These posts support the *chikari* strings and then are guided toward their respective *Khunties*.

(k) ***Parda* or frets**—Until the nineteenth century, there were sixteen frets on the sitar, but with the passage of time, the sitar acquired nineteen to twenty-one frets. These are of steel or brass. In the ancient period, the frets were called *sarikas*. In middle ages, they came to be known as *sundries*, and now we call them frets or *pardas*. When we press the string on the fret, a very resonant sound is produced of different scale on every fret. These frets are at a somewhat high level in the middle and are kept fitted on the fingerboard with silken thread or nylon string, so they are movable, thus allowing for perfect tuning. The best string for tying the frets is known as *mang* and is manufactured in Assam. All the strings pass on to these frets. The shape of the frets is one fourth of a half moon, or we could say flatly elliptical. The frets can be altered downward or upward to produce the required *swaras* of a particular scale.

(l) **Additional gourd**—Some sitars have one extra gourd at the end of the neck, where the pegs of main strings are fitted. It helps to enrich the sound of the *swaras*.

(m) **Pegs or nuts**—A standardized sitar has twenty to twenty-one pegs or *khunties* made of rose wood, four for main strings and three for *chikaries* and *Madhya Shadaj*. Seven are big pegs, and there are eleven to thirteen small pegs for the *tarabs*. The arrangement of *tarabs* allows them to be shifted so as to produce intervals of any particular scale. But nowadays, the sitars are found with five main strings, and thirteen *tarabs*.

(n) **Bead or *manka***—These oval and swan-shaped, small pieces of camel bone are pierced in all the four wires, namely *baaj ki taar* and *Jore Ki taar*, located between the *ghurach* and *langot*. The other two are put in *Kharaj* or *Laraj ki taar* and *chikari* wire located between the *pacisa* and *Khunti*. These *mankas* can be tightened or made loose accordingly to make the tuning of the required *swara*.

(o) ***Mizraab* or plectrum**—This is a hard, triangular piece of wire made to resemble a fingernail. This word is derived from Persian, meaning "to beat." It is worn on the index finger of the right hand. Dr. Lal Mani Misar has written of it in *Bhartiya Sageet Vadhya*:

> "In the ancient Granth Amarkosh, it is described as "Trikon" or three cornered, and in middle ages, it was called Nakhi or Nayika, and the same was given the name of *mizraab*".

Decoration

The typical Indian sitar has the most beautiful ornamentation. The decorations are done with antelope horn on the *tumba* and *tabli*. The grape vines, doves, or a picture of Saraswati are carved upon the *tabli*. Side decoration is done upon the corners of *tabli* and fingerboard. The decoration of bone protects the places where the *mizraab* strokes could mar the wood.

The Playing Position

There are two sitting postures for playing sitar:

1. *Sardari baithak* (sitting) Padmasan
2. *Darbari baithak*

Sardari baithak—We fold the left leg beneath the right hip and keep the right leg on the left; this is called *sardari asana*. The sitar is kept on the sole of the left foot, on the right side.

Darbari baithak—We fold both knees to our left side, and the sitar is kept on the ground, on the right side, pressed with the right elbow. The sitar's fingerboard remains bent on the left side at 60 degrees.

It should be noted that when playing the sitar one does not hold the sitar with both hands. The movement of the left-hand finger should go parallel to the thumb of the left hand, which runs on the frets. Dr. Indrani Chakarwarty writes in an essay, "Sitar Vaadan Ki Parvidhi tatha pribhashik shabdawali" in *Bhartiya Sangeet Mein Tantoo Vadhya*, by Bhanu Kumar Jain: "For women, the posture with folded knees on left side, is the best posture, though the one with left leg folded toward the right side and the right knee toward left side is also maintained by great musicians."

Wearing of the *Mizraab*

The *mizraab* is worn on the index finger of the right hand.

Right-hand position:

1. The right-hand thumb should be pressed on the last fret near the gourd. It should not move up and down while playing the sitar.
2. The *mizraab* or plectrum is worn on the index finger of the right hand and should fit on the tip of the finger tightly.

Left-hand position:

1. In sitar *vaadan*, two fingers of the left hand are used, namely the index and middle finger. The position of the fingers should be relaxed.
2. The tips of the fingers should press on the string just behind the fret and not directly on top of it, to avoid muffling of the sound.
3. The thumb should press lightly on the back of the neck in a position directly parallel to the index finger.
4. All four fingers should go together while the index finger and middle fingers run on *baaj ka taar*; the other two fingers should also stick to these. This will help in playing fast *gats* and illustrations.

Mizraab Strokes: An Analytical Study

When a stroke is given on *baaj ka taar* with the plectrum, it is called a *bol*. There have been two basic strokes from the very beginning.

1. From outside to inside: *Da*. It is called *"Aakarsh."*
2. From inside to outside: *Ra*. It is called *"Apkarsh."*
3. These two basic *bols* are of one *matra* each, that is, of one beat. But when we mix *Da+Ra*, it becomes *Dir*. So we derive the third *bol*. This *Dir* is also played in one beat. When the stroke is longer than one beat or *matra*, we put a mark of "s" This is used as a pause also.

In the fourteenth century, there were only two *bols*: *De* and *Ru*. In sitar *gats*, or compositions, *mizraab bols* play an important role. We can make as many *bols* as we wish to beautify the raga.

Here are some of the examples that have been in practice since the thirteenth century or so.

Thirteenth to Sixteenth Century

To start with, it is necessary and useful to refer to the evolutionary process of the stylistic development of raga exposition on instruments and, more particularly, the sitar. Just as the veena was originally used as accompanying instrument, so was the sitar in the initial period. When the veena became an independent solo instrument, *bols* were introduced to create highly ornamental and systematic patterns to beautify the presentations. The *bols—De, Ru, Da, Ra*—worked just as pause fillers or for accompaniment.

Sixteenth to Twentieth Century

During the eighteenth century, the *Senia* style of sitar players used different *bols* of *mizraab*, which made this instrument highly ornamental and systematic at the same time.

1. *Da   Dir   Da   Ra*

2. *Da   Ra   Dir   Da*

3. *Dir   Da   Da   Ra*

4. *Da   Ra   Da   Dir*
5. *Dir   Dir   Da   Ra*

6. *Da   Ra   Dir   Dir*

7. *Da   Dir   Dir   Dir*

8. *Da   R-Da   SR   Da*

9. *Da   SR   Da   Ra*

10. *Da   Dir   SR   Da*

11. *Da   Dir   Dir   Dir   Da   RDa   SR   Da*

12. *Da   Ra   Dir   Dir   Da   RDa   SR   Da*

13. *Dir   Da   Da   Ra   S   Dir   Da   Ra*

14.	Da	RDa	SR	Dir	Da	Dir	Da	Ra

15.	Da	Dir	Da	Da	Dir	Dir	Da	Ra

16.	Da	Dir	Dir	Da	SR	Dir	Da	Ra

17.	Da	Dir	SR	Dir	Da	Dir	Da	Ra

18.	Dir	Da	Ra	Dir	Da	Ra	Dir	Dir

19.	Da	DIr	Da	Dir	Da	Ra	Dir	Da

20.	Da	RDa	SR	Da	RDa	SR	Da	Ra

21. *Dir Da Dir Da Ra Da Da Ra Dir Da Dir Da Ra Da Da Ra*

Twentieth Century

Sitar players have made one more *bol*: *Dra*. When the *Dir* bol is played in half of the time usually taken by *Dir*, then it becomes *Dra*.

> *Dir Da Dir Da Ra Da Da Ra Dir Da Dir Da Ra Da Da Ra*

This method was considered to be highly scientific, simple, and well suited to instrumental music. Hence, it became extremely popular in North India, and in effect, it got the stamp of Maseet Khani *gat*.

Da	*Dir*	*Da*	*Ra*	*Da*	*Dir*	*Da*	*Ra*

Da	*Dir*	*Dir*	*Dir*	*Da*	*RDa*	*SR*	*Da*

This *Tukra* got the name of Raza Khani *gat*.

The *gat* presentations were developed with intelligent and full use of different *bol* patterns, forming beautiful *gats*.

Noted Maseet Khani style players during nineteenth century were Bahadur Khan, Ustad Dulhe Khan, Gulam Husain, Muglu Khan, and Pan Khan. The *Raza Khani gat* players were accomplished in playing *Thumri ang* ragas, namely *Pilu, kafi, Khamaj, Tilak Kamoj,* and *Bhairavi.* Important among *Raza Khani gat* players were Gulam Raza Khan, Ali Raza Khan, Panna Lal Vijpeyi, Babu Ishwari Parsad, Barkat Ali Khan, Saijaad Muhammad, and others. Their gats still receive the highest acclaim.

In recent times, some other strokes of mizraab have developed, which are used in *NOM TOM Ka Alap* while playing on the sitar.

Bhagwat Sharan Sharma reports in *Sitar Malika*:

"1. Dhi-na-na will be played as Da Ra Da.
2. Dhi-na-na-Dhi na-na-Dhi-na- will be played as Da Ra Da Da Ra Da Da Ra
3. Tak-Dhi-lang shall be played by mizraab as Dir Di-Ra-Ra."

So, we see there are no set rules for *mizraab* strokes. With the passage of time, many alterations have been made by the great masters. The important and only things to be considered while making *bols* are time and rhythm.

Care of the Instrument

The sitar is a very delicate instrument. Great care is needed for its handling. The old gurus worshipped the veena or other similar instruments because they were of the opinion that Ma-Saraswati is the Goddess of Sangeet, who was also called veena *vadini.*

They kept the musical instruments in a separate room along with the statue or photograph of Ma Saraswati. They lit *Dhoop-Deep* in that room. Not everyone can afford to have separate rooms for their musical instruments or sitars, but there are some things very necessary for the care of the sitar.

I visited some of the workshops where the sitar makers do their work, and I learned the following points:

1. For the long life of the *Jawari*, small piece of paper should be kept on it, so that when we are not playing, no dust particles gather on it. In this way, we don't need to change the *Jawari* every month.

2. Mustard oil is used on the strings to facilitate the smooth running of the fingers, but excess oil is harmful and if it reaches the bridge, it will spoil the voice of the sitar. To save the bridge from being spoiled, the right way is to clean the oil from the strings with cotton or a piece of soft cloth after playing.

3. The gourd of the sitar is the most delicate of all the parts. If hit by something, it can break and the voice of the sitar is spoiled, so the sitar should be kept safely intact in a box before and after use. The sitar should not be exposed for long to direct rays of the sun. A sitar should not be stored near radiators, heaters, air conditioners, or windows.

4. Do not subject the sitar to drastic and abrupt temperature changes.

I want to tell what happened when I was to give a sitar recital in Saskatoon and Abbotsford in Canada. The maximum temperature was −35°C so I had a great difficulty in taking my sitar to the theater. I wrapped my sitar first in a plastic bag, then in a blanket, and then put it in the box. But when I took it out of the box, it was as cold as ice. I sat in an air-conditioned room, and after an hour my sitar recovered. One should be very careful about the handling of the instrument.

5. When we are not playing it, the sitar should be kept in a substantial cloth bag, which covers the entire instrument. It is also a good idea to have a plastic bag made that will cover the cloth bag and keep out any moisture.

6. The sitar should be kept either lying on the floor (frets facing up) or propped in a corner (frets facing toward the corner).

Pt. Ravi Shankar ji has written in *My Music, My Life* about the care of the sitar:

> "The Sitar is such a finely made instrument that it needs a great care about each of its parts. Periodically, the tension of the strings should be relaxed. The strings should be loosened but not slacked.
>
> The sitar should be kept clean and dust free. A clean cloth can be used for wiping the exposed surfaces of the instrument. A one inch wide paint brush with two or three inches of bristle is very convenient for dusting under the strings and both bridges."

CHAPTER 4

Changing *Vaadan Shailies* of the Sitar

C hange is the law of nature. It brings beauty to the world. Without change, there is no life. This basic rule applies everywhere. The Indian sitar has seen a large application of this law of change. Many changes came in the structural form and then in *vaadan shailies*.

From the fourteenth to the eighteenth century, the method of playing the sitar was taught to the *shishyas* by their respective gurus, and the students copied the technique. There was no notation system; hence, nothing was written. Only Guru Shishya prampara continued the task. This instrument was played to supplement the other instruments. The sitarists had adopted the veena *vaadan shaily*, in which *Alaap* was given the most important place.

Historical Development of the Sitar: *Vaadan Shailies*

The historical development of the *vaadan shailies* of sitar can be viewed in three main phases:

1. *Pre-Gat* Period, fourteenth century to 1500
2. *Gat shaily* Period, 1500–1900
3. Free-form period, 1900 to present

1. Pre-*Gat* period

In this period, the sitarists played in an instrumental ensemble, complementing the *Bin* and *Rabab* (prevalent during Mughal period). The sitar's *vaadan shaily* was mostly based on vocal music and this was used to accompany *Qawwalis* and *Ghazals*. Stephen Slawek wrote on page 16 of his *Sitar Technique in Nibadha Form*: "The resonator of sitar was made of coconut shell, and the women folk played it. Simple songs of a lighter nature were played on this instrument."

Sangeet Karyala Hathras added in a comment in *Sangeet* in August 1968 (page 33): "In Ameer Khusro's period, the sitar was used only as accompaniment, i.e., for 'Sangat.' It had only two main *'bols,'* De and Ru (Sanskrit words). 'De' means 'invitation' and 'Ru' means blessings to the musician. Sitar had a very small capacity for attracting the audience, that is why it did not make much progress. The sitar *vaadan* was on the road of progress. There was not much in the *vaadan shaily*, so people did not give full attention to it."

It can be said that the sitar's voice reached the audience from the back door. It was used only as accompaniment, and the sitarist played two *bols* only—*De* and *Ru*—whenever the singer paused, so that the audience did not feel the absence of rhythm and sound.

The musicians came to know after some years that the sitar had much more capacity for solo playing, but until the beginning of the sixteenth century, this instrument was still used just as accompaniment.

During the sixteenth and seventeenth centuries, "*Dhrupad*" style was adopted by sitarists. The vocal compositions of *Dhrupad* were played and the improvisations were based on rhythmical accompaniment of the drum (*Pakhawaj*) which accompanied the *Dhrupad*. This *vaadan shaily* gave some importance to sitar.

Gat Shaily Period, 1500–1900

Two brothers. Imratsen and Nihalsen, who were Tansen's successors, had the vital roles in the progress of the sitar *vaadan* as well as in the development of the instrument itself. The brothers also put one extra gourd on the back of the *daand* in order to lengthen the "*Aass*" of the string, which helped in *Solo vaadan* of the sitar.

The *gat shaily* came into existence, we can say, in the sixteenth century, "*gat*" means *gati* in (Sanskrit) or "movement." Tansen's successors get the credit of originating the *gat shaily* and were known as "*Saini.*" The *Saini Gharana* consisted of two schools, *Binkars* and *Rababias*, which belonged to Tansen's son-in-law, Misri Khan, and his son, Bilas Khan, respectively. These musicians taught this instrument to no one else except their own family members. The *Rabab* and *Bin* playing *shaily* was included in sitar *vaadan.* They played *Alap, Jor Alap*, and compositions that were popular in vocal music at that time. These compositions came to be known as *gats*. This period can be called as the start of the *gat shaily* period.

During this same time, Sadarang made *Khayal Gayaki* popular, which was followed also by the sitar. The *vilambit khayal* played on the sitar was known as *Vilambit gat*, which Maseet Khan created. The compositions (*gats*) were based on fixed *mizraab bols* and in specific tempos. These *vilambit gats* came to be known as Maseet Khani *gats*. This *vaadan shaily* was known as Delhi *baaj* also, because Maseet Khan resided in Delhi.

In the sixteenth century, some sitarists played Raza Khani *gats* created by Ghulam Raza Khan. This *gat shaily* was based on the *Thumri* and *Tarana* styles of vocal music. These *gats* were played at very fast tempos, whereas the Maseet Khani *gats* were slow in tempo, so the player could do a lot by playing of *toraas, soot, gamak, ghaseet*, and *meend*.

The Raza Khani *gats* were then succeeded by sitar *khani gats*, which were performed after Raza Khani *gats* to show more rhythm, color, and sweetness of the composition. The *Vilambit gat* and *Drut gats* became greatly popular among the sitarists during the nineteenth century.

Free-Form Period, 1900 to Present

The styles that are played on sitar in the twenty-first century have their origins from the old *vaadan shailies*, such as *Alap, Jor-alaap, Dhrupad, Khayal,* Maseet Khani, Raza khani *baaj*, sitar Khani *gats,* Ameer Khani *gats, khayal shaily* of vocal music, classical music, and light music compositions, which include *thumri, dadra, tappa, ghazal, bhajan* and *lok geets,* and folk tunes. All these mixtures have given birth to a new style, which the current sitarists created on their own because they wanted to follow their own tastes, although some hard and fast rules are still obeyed while playing classical ragas, but even those are being replaced with "*mishrit ragas.*" So, it seems there will be no rules when pure, free-form playing will be adopted by the sitarists. The sitarist will be free to express his mood in *swaras*.

The details of all the phases of sitar *vaadan shail*es are given below.

As there was no notation system before the twentieth century, we don't have any written records about the *vaadan shailies* of those periods. As the records show, there have been some very renowned musicians who have contributed a lot toward the development of the sitar and its techniques as well as the *vaadan shaily*.

Ustaad Raheem Sen and Amrit Sen were great musicians of the nineteenth century, who made great changes in sitar *vaadan shaily* and added beauty and rhythm to it.

Ustaad Raheem Sen—1813,nineteenth century
According to Bhagwat Sharan Sharma in *Sitar Malika*: "He learnt the art from Dulhe Khan, his father-in-law. No one gave any importance to this instrument but Raheem Sen continued his riaz and put all the techniques of veena, *Dhrupad*, Dhamar and Khayal gayaki into the sitar vaadan. He is remembered for making this instrument popular among the people of that time."
Amrit Sen—1813-1893
Bhagwat Sharan Sharma also records in *Sitar Malika*: "Amrit Sen was born in 1813. He got support from Jaipur Naresh, Maharaja Ramsingh. Amrit Sen had the wonderful capacity to play sitar until months together. He died in the year 1893 in Jaipur. But it is shocking, we don't get any records of written compositions."
Raza Khan and Maseet Khan—These two great musicians made Raza Khani or Drut *gats* and Maseet Khani or *Vilambit gats,* respectively. They developed solo *vaadan* in sitar. These two types of *gats* were played separately by the sitarists, comprising of *alaap, Jor alaap, drut gat, toraas* and then *jhala*.

For this *vaadan shaily*, these two musicians made some changes in the structural form of sitar. They set twenty-three frets on *Achal thaat* sitar and kept seven strings, which were tuned as:

1. *Ma*
2. *Sa*
3. *Sa (Jore ki Taars)*
4. *Pa*
5. *Pa*
6. *Sa*
7. *Sa*

Sahabdad Khan (19th Century)—Another scholar, Sahabdad Khan, contributed a great deal to the sitar *vaadan*. He invented one new instrument, the *"Sur-bahar,"* on which he played *Alaap* with *meend*. Because the strings of this instrument were thick, the *sur-bahar* recital showed the sensitive notes (*gambheer swaras*) beautifully. The playing of *Alaap* with *meend, gamak* was done on *sur bahar* while the raga *gat* was played on the sitar.

Imdad Khan—He promoted and developed the sitar *vaadan shaily* in his own way. He was of the opinion that *meend* was the most important and beautiful part in sitar *vaadan*, and an ornament of the raga.

In Raza Khan's and Maseet Khan's period, the field of music was not so wide and vast because there were twenty-three frets in the *Achal thaat* sitar, which made it difficult for the player to produce *meend*. But Imdad Khan kept only nineteen frets and named that sitar as *Chal thaat* sitar. He performed the *meend* of four *swaras* on the sitar and seven *swaras meend* on the *Surbahar.*

Imdad Khan added the *tarb* strings to the sitar, which increased the *Ass* of the main string, that is, the sound of the main string increased. And now we can't even imagine a sitar without *tarbs*.

Inayat Khan (1882–1927)—Imdad Khan's son, Inayat Khan, attached one extra gourd on the upper part of the *daand*, which also helped in making the sound of the sitar more resonant and sweet. He stressed the use of *meend, gamak,* and *kan swara* in the sitar *vaadan*. So, this *vaadan shaily* attracted much more of an audience than before. This *shaily* was widely adopted by the musicians of that period. The *gats* fitted the tastes of the people. The folk tunes had become popular in sitar *vaadan*, because they depicted different cultures and the beauty of individual tribes. *Dhrupads,* *alaap,* and *Jor Alaap* were the basic parts that the sitarist of that period played, wherever there was an occasion for instrumental music.

An Analytical Study of Changing *Vaadan Shailies* of the Sitar

The sitar that we use today is the same as was played in Imdad Khan's period. He improved the quality of *Jawari* also, and that is why the voice of the sitar was improved. The whole credit goes to Imdad Khan Saheb for the improvement in the *tarab* strings of the sitar.

The changes in the structural form and *vaadan shailies* go together. Whenever the sitarist wanted to change *swaras,* he put on or took off one or another of the strings.

Inayat Khan's son, Vilayat Khan, made some changes in the main strings. He lessened the number of strings. Instead of seven, he used five, but after more thought, he placed one more string, which was tuned into *Mandra Sa.* Then he took off one *Jore*-string and put one copper string, which was tuned into the *vaadi swara* of the raga to be played.

Pt. Ravi Shankar ji replaced the *Jore* string with a string tuned to *Kharaj*: thus, he increased the range of sitar *vaadan* up to four *saptaks* in *alaap.*

The *Gat* which had come into existence in the sixteenth century, was improved by Imratsen and Nihalsen. Although it was not accomplished with today's tabla or *Pakhawaj* beats, there was a tinge of *Dhrupad vaadan shaily. Alap ang* was very powerful.

The right hand was used more than the left hand. The *mizraab bols* were the most important part of the *vaadan shaily.*

From this Guru Shishya Prampara, we had two great musicians— Maseet Khan and Raza Khan of Lucknow.

Maseet Khani *gat shaily*—This shaily was introduced by Maseet Khan and came to be known as Delhi *baaj* also. The Maseet Khani *gats* had the following *bols* of *mizraab*:

Dir   Da   Dir   Da   Ra   Da   Da   Ra

Dir   Da   Dir   Da   Ra   Da   Da   Ra = 16 beats.

These strokes had so much beauty of rhythm that they are used widely even today. These *gats* were *vilambit gats*.

Raza Khani *gat shaily*—The second *vaadan shaily* was started by Raza Khan of Lucknow. He originated *Khayal* and *Thumri ang* in sitar *vaadan*. These were fast tempo *gats*. This *vaadan shaily* was known as *Poorvi Baaj* also. In these *gats*, small pieces in fast *laya* were played, such as *drut gats* with elaborations.

Dhruvpad *shaily*—This *shaily* became important in the eighteenth century because of Tansen's successors, Amritsen and Nihalsen. They popularized the Maseet Khani and Raza Khani *gats*. Amritsen's father was a great sitarist. He played *alap* and *jor-alap* on the sitar with perfection. Amritsen received his instructions from his father and became a famous sitar player. He followed his father's *vaadan shaily*, that is, *Dhruvpad* style. This *vaadan shaily* made the instrument popular among the people of that time, and they loved to hear its resonant sound.

Ameer Khani *gat shaily*—Pt. Jaagdish Narayan Pathak in *Sangeet Shastar Mimansa*, 1968, wrote about Ameer Khan: "One of the successors of Amritsen named Ameer Khan (1873–1914) also earned fame in this field. He made one separate *vaadan shaily* which came to be known as Ameer Khani *gat shaily*. In this *shaily* the *gats* were played in *madhya laya*. The *mizraab* strokes or *bols* were the same as of Maseet Khani *gat*, i.e.,

Dir	*Da*	*Dir*	*Da*	*Ra*	*Da*	*Da*	*Ra*
Dir	*Da*	*Dir*	*Da*	*Ra*	*Ra*	*Da*	*Ra* = 16 beats

The difference was only of beats that these *bols* were of eight matras and were played only once. It means that the Madhya *laya gats* were of eight beats only."

This *vaadan shaily* was known as *Jaipuri Baaj* also. This *vaadan shaily* had perfect *Jor* and *Alaap*. In the line of successors, there were some of the noted sitar players.

Bhagwat Sharan Sharma wrote in *Sitar Malika*: "Imdad Khan had the perfection for playing seven *swaras meend* on Sitar as well as on Surbahar, and was a perfect sitar player. His son Inayat Khan continued his efforts in making sitar playing popular. He was called 'Avtaar' in sangeet Jagat (world of music). He was a genius and played beautiful *gat*, Toraas and *Jhala* on Sitar."

Shri Khusi Ram Bedi wrote in his essay, "Bhaarat ke Bade Gharanon Ki Sitarkari aur Taaleem," published in the book *Sitar Shiksha*: "Ustaad Inayat Khan's son Ustaad Vilayat Khan made his contributions toward artistic layakaris, *Jod-alaap*, *gat* and *toraas*."

The other innovation in *vaadan shailies* of sitar was made by Ustaad Alaudin Khan. He mixed *Khyal Ang* and *Dhrupad* in sitar *vaadan*. It was he who put the *Anumandra Alaapchaari* of veena into sitar *vaadan* and it became a new *vaadan shaily*.

As Bhagvat Sharan Sharma wrote in *Sitar Malika*: "The Sain Vanshiya Shaily was somewhat difficult, though interesting. So as the instrument got name and fame, the common man came forward to learn the Maseet Khani *gats* because these *gats* were in slow rhythm, simple and based on Khayal Ang."

In the nineteenth century, *thumri* and *ghazal* had the main influences on sitar *vaadan* and a new *vaadan shaily* came into existence. *Drut gats* were made in which *taans* and *jhala* work was appreciable. The *vilambit gats* were of two types:

Senia *gats*
Maseet Khani *gats*

Senia *gats*—Sharma wrote of the Senia gats: "In these *gats*, there was a set place for starting any composition, set place means some specific matra. For '*toraas*,' '*tihai*,' or '*tiyas*' no definite rules were adopted, so the tabla player had to face a great difficulty to have the rapport with the sitar player. '*Sam*' has an important role and place in sitar *vaadan* or any kind of music, but because these *gats* had confusion surrounding this, these could not gain popularity."

Maseet Khani *gats*—A Maseet Khani *gat* started from the twelfth *matra* and was played in *teen taal* only. The use of *meend* and *gamak* was done with perfection. The same style or *vaadan shaily* is also prevalent today. The *bols* are the same. The nineteenth-century *gats* had four parts:

1. *Sthai*
2. *Antra*
3. *Sanchari*
4. *Aabhog*

But now, only *Sthai* and *Antra* are played in *Vilambit* as well as in *Drut gats*. After these two parts, *toraas* or *taans* are played with different *matras*. The fourth place comes for *jhala*.

Nowadays, the sitar player plays the *alaap, jor alaap,* short *jhala* of the raga, and then comes the *Vilambit gat* with *toraas* of different *matras* or beats. After this, the artist starts *drut gat* and when *sthai* and *antra* are finished, *toraas* or *taans* are played. Then comes the turn of *jhala*, which is the height of rhythm.

In the nineteenth century, Imdad Khan made his impact on society in the field of music. He made different tunes with different *mizraab bols* and strokes and originated another *shaily* in *jhala* playing. We get to know only theoretically that these musicians made such and such *vaadan shaily*. Due to the lack of notation system, nothing is available of the precious property, which got buried with the past artists. The only sources are persons who tell us the story of their *Gharana* or the *shailies* present in their *Gharana*.

Imdad Khan's son, Inayat Khan, made the "*Bandish*" of the raga, with *toraas*. This method was easy for the beginners. *Tiya* or *Tihai* was started by Inayat Khan Sahib. In this period, there was another sitarist named Babu Khan, who stressed free and imaginative *toraas* of the raga and with true *swaras* of the raga.

In the Sangeet Karyalya Hathras publication, Sangeet wrote of this: "While Ashique Ali Khan Sahib was famous for his melodic ragas, Haider Hussain Khan made the *Dir Dir bols* and Yusuf Ali Khan was famous for his effective *gats*."

Until the year 1950, the sitar playing was done with different *gat karees* like Maseet Khani *gat* or Raza Khani *gat*. The tabla was played with sitar, and the *Khyal gayaki* method or *shaily* was adopted with the decoration of *meend, gamak, kan swara,* and *murkies*.

Vilayat Khan, son of Inayat Khan, added *gayaki ang*, so a new *vaadan shaily* was born.

The role of the left hand increased, and a *meend* of five *swaras* was produced. With the advent of this new *vaadan shaily,* the *gayaki ang* became popular.

So we reach the conclusion that from fourteenth century to 1500, the sitar was used as accompaniment and *swara vistaars*; then, it became popular for its solo *vaadan*.

From 1500 to 1900—The great sitarist Amritsen made beautiful *gats*. Maseet Khani or *Vilambit gats* and Raza Khani or *Drut Gats* had developed, and these two musicians made great contribution toward the existing *vaadan shaily* of the sitar. These *gats* are the soul of sitar *vaadan*. They are based on *khayal gayaki*, folk tunes, or according to the raga only.

Gats were played with the ornamentation of *meend* and *gamak*. *Toraas* of different style and of different *matras* were added to beautify the *gat*.

Because the *bols* of Maseet Khani *gat* were played according to set rules, they were simple for the learners and that was the reason for their popularity. The *been shaily* was also put into sitar *vaadan*. The great musician Sada Rang started the *khayal shaily*, which people liked. Although this style was based mainly on *Geet*, the *Bandish* took the name of *Gat*. Whereas in Delhi, the Maseet Khani *gat vaadan shaily* was becoming popular, the Raza Khani *gat shaily* was at the peak of its popularity in Lucknow.

So, these two *gat shailies* were the only ones that received the name in history of Indian classical and light instrumental music. Maseet Khani *gat shaily* is cool and calm. The Raza Khani *gat shaily* forced the audience to dance to its tunes.

Twentieth century—Change is a principle of the cycle of life that holds true with music also. After 1900, a new *vaadan shaily* was born that allowed the artists to express free will but with some of the basic ties.

The sitarists started playing the sitar as follows:

1. *Alaap* with *Dhruvpad ang.*
2. *Jor alaap.*
3. Maseet Khani *gat* with *toraas* or *taans.*
4. Raza Khani *gat* with *toraas* or *taans.*
5. *Jhala* with *toraas.*

Now the sitarist is not bound to play the *gat* in *teen-taal* only, but he is free to play whatever he wants or whichever *vaadan shaily* he wants to adopt. He may play *Thumri, Dadra, Tappa, Bhajan, Ghazal* tunes or even a folk tune.

There is no compulsion as to how, when, and which *vaadan* is to be done. It solely depends upon the sitarist to choose the time, raga, the style of playing any *cheez* or *tukra*.

Alaap and *Jor-alaap* are done so beautifully on sitar these days that *surbahar* instrument is vanishing. The artist is free to compose any tune based on the *swaras* of any raga or the composition can be of a folk song.

Basic Rules to Form a Composition

The basic techniques remain the same as were prevalent from the fourteenth to the nineteenth century, which are:

- There should be rapport between the sitar and tabla player.
- *Sam* is a must, otherwise the tabla accompanist is lost somewhere and the rhythmic chain breaks.
- A *gat* must contain *sthai, antra, toraas,* and *Jhala.*
- Maseet Khani *gat* is to be played in *teentaal* and Raza Khani *gat* can be played in any of the *talas* according to the taste of the artist and tune of the *gat.*

Changing Strokes of the Mizraab
(Historical Survey)

After we have discussed in detail the changing *vaadan shailies* of the sitar, we must go through the changing strokes of *mizraab* used in all these *gat shailies*. There has been no change in the strokes of *mizraab* of Maseet Khani and Raza Khani *gats*.

1. Bols of Maseet Khani *gat shaily:*

x				2				0			3				
1	2	3	4	5	6	7	8	9	10	11	12	13	14	15	16
											Dir	Da	Dir	Da	Ra

Da Da Ra Dir Da Dir Da Ra Da Da Ra

2. Bols of Raza Khani *gat shaily* (nineteenth century): These started from the ninth matra:

x				2				0				3			
1	2	3	4	5	6	7	8	9	10	11	12	13	14	15	16
								Da	Dir	Da	Ra	Da	Dir	Da	Ra

Da Dir Dir Dir Da RDa SR Da

Over time, the artists started the *gat* from the seventh matra:

x				2				0				3			
1	2	3	4	5	6	7	8	9	10	11	12	13	14	15	16
						Dir	Dir	Da	RDa	SR	Da	Da	Dir	Da	Ra

Da S S Ra Da Ra

There has been an era of another *gat shailies* also, which are no longer prevalent. The *mizraab* strokes of those *gat shailies* were:

3. Sitar Khani *gat shaily*:

x			2				
1	2	3	4	5	6	7	8
Da	*Dir*	*Dir*	*Dir*	*Da*	*RDa*	*SR*	*Da*

These *gats* were played in *Adha taal*, i.e., Panjabi *Theka*, which was as follows:

x			2				0			3					
1	2	3	4	5	6	7	8	9	10	11	12	13	14	15	16
Dha	*S*	*Dhin*	*Dha*	*Dha*	*S*	*Dhin*	*Dha*	*Dha*	*S*		*Tin*	*Ta*	*Ta*	*S*	*Dhin*	*Dha*

4. Zaafar Khani *gat shaily*: Zaafar Khan belonged to Tansen's *Saini Gharana*. He was a veena player. This *vaadan shaily* was adopted by sitarists.

The *mizraab* strokes were:

1	2	3	4
Da	Dra	DaRa	Da

The sitarists of this *vaadan shaily* played *murkies* also on the sitar for the beautification of the *gat*.

5. Kut-baj *gat shaily*: The *bols* of *mizraab* were at the discretion of the sitarist. If the *gat* was in *Dadra Taal*, the *bols* were:

Da	Dir	Da	Da	Dir	Da

If the *gat* was in another *taal*, the pieces were arranged in that *taal*.

Stephen M. Swalek, in his book *Sitar Technique in Nibadh Forms*, wrote: "The term 'Kut-baj' is applied to those *gats* that are composed in talas other than teen-taal, regardless of the *laya*. These *gats* follow the same structural principle of sectionalization. A common feature of kut-baj *gats* is that their mizraab-*bols* patterns are usually governed by the divisions of the taal in which they are composed."

Mizraab bols of *Kut-baj*

Jhaptaal 2 - 3 - 2 - 3

1	2	3	4	5	6	7	8	9	10
Da	Ra	Da	Da	Ra	Dir	Da	Rda	Da	Ra
x		2			0		3		

Ek-taal 2 - 2 - 2 - 2

1	2	3	4	5	6	7	8	9	10	11	12
Da	—	Da	Dir	Da	Ra	Da	Dir	Da	Ra	Da	Ra
x		0		2		0		3		4	

Roopak taal

1	2	3	4	5	6	7
Da	Da	Ra	Da	Ra	Da	Ra
x			1		2	

6. Ameer Khani *gat shaily*: This *shaily* used the technique of Maseet Khani *gats*, but was played in *Madhya Laya*, so it could not be successful.

Here is a list of the many changes in the *vaadan shailies* of the sitar from the thirteenth century until now:

1. The sitar was used as an accompaniment in the thirteenth century with only two strokes of *mizraab*: *"De" "Ru" or "Da" "Ra."*
2. The sitar adopted the veena's *alaap ang*.
3. *Sur bahar's geet ang* was put into the sitar *vaadan*.
4. The *Dhrupad Khayal shaily* was adopted by sitarists, which was started by Amrit Sen.
5. The Khayal Gayan *shaily* was put into sitar *vaadan*, with which *swara vistaar* increased.
6. The use of right and left hand had equal importance, whereas from the thirteenth century to the seventeenth century, the *mizraab* strokes and the right-hand movement had the main role. The right hand made beautiful *mizraab* strokes, while the left hand produced sweet sounds of *swaras*.
7. The *meend* and *gamak* work increased.
8. Maseet Khani and Raza Khani *gats* came into existence between the eighteenth and ninetenth century.
9. The *meend* of two *swaras* to five *swaras*, then to seven *swaras*, was ably produced. Ustaad Raheem Khan, a disciple of Ustaad Imdad Khan, played seven *swaras meend* with great ability. Buddhaditya Mukerjee also plays seven *swaras meend*.
10. The *alaap* and *Jor* were played on the *surbahar*, while the *gat* and *toraas* were played on the sitar. The *gat* had *sthai, Antra, Sanchaari,* and *Aabhog* as its parts.
11. *Tiya* or *Tihai* was started by Inayat Khan, which created beauty of rhythm.

12. Pt. Ravi Shankar ji originated many things in sitar *vaadan*, which has brought total perfection to this instrument.
13. *Alaapchaari, meend, gamak,* Kan *swara, Krintan, ghaseet,* and *zamzama* are some of the techniques that Pt. Ravi Shankar ji has put into sitar *vaadan*.

Now, the sitar is a perfect instrument for classical as well as for light music. It has the depth of *swaras* in the shape of *Alaap ang* and beauty in the light *gats*. Pt. Ravi Shankar ji's devotion toward music has made this instrument more popular among the people of other countries as well.

The *mizraab* strokes have made the sitar *vaadan* interesting, and the tune of an old song could be in the language or *bols* of sitar as written below:

Uth Jaa gMu sa fir Bho r Bh ee Ab Rai nKa han Jo So wat Hai

8 beats | 8 beats

Dir Da Dir Da Ra Da Da Ra | Dir Da Dir Da Ra Da Da Ra

Changing Styles in *Jhala* Playing

Meaning of *Jhala*

Jhala is a technique that shows rhythm at its heights. Its *mizraab* strokes are *Da Ra Ra Ra* or *Da Ra Ra Da | Ra Ra Da Ra*. Many musicians believe that *Jhala* originated with the imitation of a specific class of *Pakhawaj bols* known as *Tapiya*, which consisted of such pattern as *Ge Na Na Na Ge Na Na Na*, etc. which became *mizraab bols*.

In veena *vaadan*, the *jhala* is played after *alaap ang* and not after *Bandish*. But in the sitar, the tradition has been different. It is played after *jor alaap* and then after fast *gat*'s *toraas*.

Pt. Gopal Krishan ji, the renowned veena player, also adopted the old style; that is, he played *jhala* after *jor-alaap*.

In an interview at Chandigarh, on January 25, 1990, he told me that in *Vichitra* veena, the *Jhala* seems beautiful if it is played after *jor-alaap*.

Presently, the sitarist plays the full raga on sitar and after the *toraas* of fast *gat*, *jhala* is played, which shows the energy, rhythm, beauty, and full bloom of that raga.

Jhala has been of two types from the beginning of the twentieth century and even now the old system prevails, although with a few changes. It is now used primarily as a concluding section in *drut gat*.

1. Simple or *Seedha Jhala*
2. Reverse or *Ulta Jhala*

1. Simple *Jhala*—In simple *jhala*, *Da bol* is played with the stroke of *mizraab* on *Baaj ki taar* and *Ra bol* is played on the *chikari* string, i.e., *Da Ra Da Ra*. These four strokes make one unit.

2. Reverse *Jhala*—In this process, we start from the *Re bol* on *chikari*, then *Da* on the *Baaj* string, and again *Ra* two times on the *chikari*. It goes like this: *Ra Da Ra Ra*. One can play as many techniques as one likes.

Some of the kinds played are:

Simple *Jhala*

1. *Da Ra Ra Ra*, repeat four times (basic technique).
2. *Da Ra Ra Da, Ra Ra Da Ra, Da Da Ra Ra, Da Ra Da Ra*
3. *Da Ra Ra Da, Ra Ra Da Da, Da Ra Ra Da, Ra Ra Da Ra*
4. *Da Ra Ra Ra, Da Ra Ra Ra, Da Ra Da Ra, Da Ra Da Ra*
5. *Da Ra Da Ra, Da Ra Da Ra, Da Ra Da Ra, Da Ra Da Ra*
6. *Da Ra Ra Da, Ra Da Ra Ra, Da Ra Ra Da, Ra Da Da Ra*

Reverse *Jhala*

1. *S Da S S, S Da S S, S Da S S, S Da S S*
2. *S S S S, S Da S Da, S S S S, S Da S Da*
3. *S S S Da, S Da S Da, S S S Da, S Da S Da*
4. *S Da S Da, S S S S, S Da S Da, S S S S*

The reverse *jhala* is not in use much. The simple *jhala* is much more beautiful than the reverse *jhala* or ulta *Jhala*.

Alaap—This is the most important part of the raga. To introduce the raga there is a passage of notes without rhythm, which is called *Alaap*. The sitarist goes into the depth of the nature of the notes used in a particular raga, and he tries to produce all the *rasas* that are related to that particular *swara* in that particular raga.

As in Raga Bhairavi, *Re Ga Dha Ni* flat notes are used. The flat note has a very sensitive and serious nature. The artist tries to cooperate with that mood and treats every *swara* with a soft feeling, so that the *swara* also expresses itself with much interest. In this way, there begins a rapport between the artist and the *swaras* of that raga. The whole of the raga is introduced by the notes of that raga in *Alaap*.

Pt. Sharangdev has written of this in Sangeet Ratnakar: "Where Greh, Ansh, Mandra, Taar, Audattava, Shaddattava, Alpattava, Bahuttava, Nayas, Apnyas, raga laxans are shown, that system is called 'Raga-*Alaap*.'"

The *Bandish,* or the tune, constructs the outer appearance of the raga, whereas *Alaap* is the soul of the raga. The beauty of the raga is centered in its *Alaap*. It can be called the base on which the raga is constructed. It is considered to be the supreme test of a musician's creativity. From the very beginning of the twentieth century, *Alaap* was played to decorate the raga. In the beginning, it had four parts:

1. *Sthai*
2. *Antra*
3. *Sanchari*
4. *Aabhog*

1. In the first form of *jhala*, the sitarist plays on the Mandra Saptak's *swaras* and finishes on Madhya Saptak's "*Sa*" note. Every ending is done with a *Mukhra*, which is a section of a few *swaras* played in rhythm.
2. In this stage, the player begins the *Alaap* from *Madhya Shadaj* and goes to *Taar Shadaj*.
3. The player uses high-pitched notes, such as from *Taar Shadaj* to *Taar Pancham*.
4. At this stage, the artist shows all the *swaras* of the raga by playing *meend, kan swar,* etc. All the three *saptaks* are touched so that the whole *swaroop* of the raga is repeated to the audience.

Nowadays, not all musicians cover the last two stages, because this tradition is old one. In second stage only, the sitarist goes up to *Taar saptak* and returns to *Madhya Shadaj*. The most important place in playing *Alaap* in *Antra* is its beginning, as to how it is started. Usually, it starts from *Gandhaar* or *Madhyam* of *Madhya saptak*.

Notation Symbols

Meaning of Notation

Notation is the representation of music through written symbols. Its use for increasing one's repertoire is claiming greater acceptability instead of serving merely as a reference or as a written memory.

According to the *Encyclopedia Britannica*: "Notation is a graphic method of representing sounds to the ear through the medium of the eye."

Nikhil Ghosh writes in *Fundamentals of Raga and Tala with a New System of Notation*: "Notation, as a musical term, means the system of writing music by signs and symbols to represent the pitch, duration, rise and fall of musical sounds."

To preserve all the properties of sitar *vaadan*, there must be some source. We are lucky enough that Pt. Vishnu Narayan Bhaat Khande invented one notation system, "*Padawati*," that could preserve the things as they existed at the time. Without such a system, we would have lost thousands of valuable *vaadan shailies* and their system or notations, without which no raga composition or any other *vaadan* could be traced out. Pt. Bhaat Khande ji devised symbols that are used while writing anything played or sung by the artists.

Pt. Vishnu Narayan Bhaat Khande Swara Lipi Padwati

Sr.	Name	Symbol	Placement	Explanation
1.	*Shudh Swara* or natural note	No sign	*Sa Re Ga Ma Pa Dha Ni*	In Hindustani *sangeet* there are basic seven *swaras*, which are equivalent of the Western Do, Re, Mi, Fa, So, La, Ti

2.	*Komal* or Flat notes	—	<u>Re</u> <u>Ga</u> <u>Dha</u> <u>Ni</u>	When a note is played half a tone lower than the *shudh* note, it is called a flat note. The eighth, fourteenth, eighteenth and nineteenth frets are to be moved back toward the main tuning pegs.
3.	*Tiwra Swar*	*I*	*M*	This *swara* is half a tone higher than the *Shudh Ma*. This symbol appears only on *Ma swar*.
4.	Rest or Pause	*S* or —	*Sa-Re-Ga-Ma* or *Sa S S Re*.	These rests or pauses are of equal duration. The finger should not be lifted from the string during rest or pause period.
5.	*Matra*		<u>SaRe</u> <u>GaMa</u>	This is a metrical unit of one beat.
6.	Octave			
(a)	*Mandra*	*B i n d u* under the *swara*	.*Ni* .*Dha* .*Pa* .*Ma* .*Ga*	(a) When the dot appears below the note, it is played in lower octave.
(b)	*Madhya*	No sign	*Sa Re Ga Ma Pa Dha Ni*	(b) These are *shudh swaras*, called *Madhaya saptak swaras*.
(c)	*Taar*	*B i n d u* above the note	*Sa. Re.Ga.Ma.*	(c)When the dot appears above the note, it is played in the upper octave.
			X	
7.	*Sum*	X	1 2 3 4 5 6 7 8	It is the most important place of the beat where the tabla player and the sitar player meet on the rhythmic cycle's first beat. It is indicated by hand beats also.

			X **2** **3**	
8.	*Tali*	1, 2, 3, 4	1 2 3 | 4 5 | 6 7	*Tali* is indicated by hand beat. Apart from *Sum, talies* are given the main stress.
9.	*Khali*	0	0 9 10 11 12	It is called empty beat and is shown by a wave of the right hand.
10.	*Chikari*	*C or S*	*Sa C Re C or Sa S S S Re S S*	It indicates the *Ra* stroke of *mizraab* on the sitar's *chikari* string, and is used for filling the gap of equal duration and for *jhala*, a kind of *vaadan* in a sitar recital after one has played fast *gat* with *toraas*.
11.	*Krintan*		*Dha Pa Ni Dha Sa Ni Re Sa*	When we place the second finger of the left hand on *Dha swara*, and the first finger on *Pa swara*, the *mizraab* stroke should be done in *Da* form, where we pluck the string on the *Dha* fret and then on *Pa*. The repetition of next *swaras* will produce *Krintan*.
12.	*Murki*		*Sa Re Ga Ma*	When more than one note is produced in only one stroke of *mizraab*, it is called *Murki*.

13. *Kampan*	—	*Sa*	When the stroke of *mizraab* is given to a particular *swara* softly with the index finger of the left hand, it is called *Kampan*.
14. *Zamzama*	—	*Re Sa Re Sa*	This pattern makes the groupings. When two notes are played in quick succession in one stroke of *mizraab*, then the voice produced is called *zamzama*. When the symbol is like one peak upon *swaras*, these are to be played once and when there are two peaks, these are to be played thrice. The sound created by this technique is called *Zamzama*.
15. *Pukar*	*0 0 0*	*Sa .Ni .Dha Sa. Ni Dha*	When two or three *saptaks* or octaves are played in succession, it is called *pukar*.

16.	*Gamak* or grace note	—	*Ga Ma Ga Ma*

When we pull the strings from one note to the other and come back on the same note, this process creates *Gamak* or grace note. There are fifteen types of *gamaks* written in Indian music books but they are not in use these days. Pt. Sharangdev writes about a *gamak* as, "*Swrassay Kampo Gamakah*" (i.e., to vibrate the *swara* means *gamak*).

17.	*Meend*	—	*Sa Pa*

By pulling a note on the string, another *swara* is produced without touching any other note in between them. This is called *Meend* because this process brings two *swaras* together; it is called *Jor* also. We can take *meend* of more than two *swaras* also. From the time of *gat Shally,* meend work has progressed.

It has made the sitar *vaadan* very popular because the player can do the *gayaki ang* on it very efficiently because of *meend.*

18. *Kan Swara*	—	*Sa Re*	When we touch another *swara* while pressing one particular *swara* on that fret, the sound created is called *Kan swara*, meaning touch of another swara.
19. *Soot or Ghaseet*		*Sa Pa* *Sa Pa*	When the sitarist goes straight toward a distant *swara* without producing the mid *swaras*, this process is known as *Ghaseet* or *soot* (i.e., *Re Pa Pa Ni Dha Sa*).
20. *Gitakari*	—	*Ra Sa Ni Sa Dha Pa Ma Pa*	In one stroke of *mizraab*, three or four *swaras* are played in *chakkar daar* technique, which is called *Gitkari*. But this technique has changed to more *mizraab* strokes. The artist plays the notes with four strokes of *mizraab* if he is doing the *gitkari* work (means laying four *swaras* in ascending and descending order).
21. *Jhala*	*S S S S*	*Sa S S S* *Re S S S*	In sitar playing, another thing of beauty is *Jhala* when the *Ra bol* is played three times on the *chikari* string; the process is known as *Jhala*.

Pt. Bhaat Khande gets the credit for the collection of old treasures from great musicians and he made the notations, and then wrote a book named *Kramik Pustak Malika*. He invented this *swara lipi padwati,* and now anyone can sing or play anything on the sitar after studying the notation. The notation system has made Indian music easy.

Sitarists Who Have Enriched the Instrument

Thirteenth to Fourteenth Century—Ameer Khusro (1285–1351)

He gave the name of *Seh-taar* to the *Tri-tantri* veena, which was played as an accompaniment to vocal music with the *bols Da-Ra.*

Sixteenth Century—Ustad Bilaas Khan Sahib

Before the sixteenth century, there was no solo sitar *vaadan.* Ustad Bilaas Khan Sahib used the sitar for solo *vaadan* and composed some *gats* in *teen taal.*

Sixteenth Century—Raj Ras Khan Sahib or Firoz Khan

He made Firoz Khani *gats* with fast tempo, but these *gats* were overshadowed by Maseet Khani *gats,* which were composed by Maseet Khan in the late sixteenth century or the beginning of the seventeenth century.

Sixteenth Century—Maseet Khan (*Beenkar* and Sitarist)

He originated Maseet Khani *gats* based on *dhrupad* and *been* style. These *gats* were in slow tempo.

Sixteenth Century—Bahadur Khan

He was son of Ustaad Maseet Khan. Bahadur Khan composed *gat* and *toraas* for the sitar.

Sixteenth Century—Raza Khan

The *gats* introduced by Ustaad Raza Khan are known as Raza Khani *gats.* These *gats* are based on *Thumri, Tarana,* and to some extent *khayal. Piloo, Kafi, Khamaj, Tilak-Kamod, Bhairavi, Desh, and Sohni* are examples of ragas that come alive with *Thumri ang* in them.

Sixteenth Century 1516–1585 Tansen's Shishya Prampara

Suratsen	Tarangsen	Sharatsen	Vilas Khan	Saraswati

Note:Seventeenth Century—No history of any sitarists is available because of so many attacks by the foreigners.

Eighteenth Century—Ustaad Dulhe Khan

Gulam Hussain Khan Ustaad Bahadur Khan

Pan Khan Maghu Khan

Nineteenth Century (1813)

Ustaad Surat Sen

Ustaad Raheem Sen

Ustaad Raheemsen brought all the techniques of *been, dhrupad,* and *Khayal gayaki* to the sitar.

(1813–1893) **Ustaad Amrit Sen**

Ustaad Nihalsen (grandson of Ustaad Amrit Sen)

Zafar Khan

The *gats,* which came to be known as Zafar Khani *gats,* were composed by Ustaad Zafar Khan, but we know only the name of ustaads and the *gats.* No details of the *gats* or compositions are available.

Nineteenth Century (1814–1873)—Ustaad Ameer Khan

He was a *Beenkar* and *Dharupdia.* He introduced Ameer Khani *baaj* on the basis of Maseet Khan's *gats.*

(1851–1926)—Ustaad Vazeer Khan Sahib
He played to perfection in *Vilambit laya gats* and was a follower of Maseet Khan Sahib.

(1841–1895)—Sh. Krishan Rav, Raghunath Rav
These two brothers were great sitarists of their time, but we don't have the exact dates. They perfected *vilambit laya gats*.

Ustaad Sahabdad Khan Sahib
He was a great sitarist, who passed all his talent to his two sons, who also became the pillars of the sitar in Indian classical music.

Twentieth Century (1848–1920)
Ustaad Imdad Khan - Ustaad Karimdad Khan
Gayaki ang   *Gayaki ang*

These two brothers set rules for Indian classical music as well as for light classical instrumental music.

Ustaad Imdad Khan became so popular in the world of Indian instrumental music that his style came to be known as Imdad Khani style. He put *gayaki ang* in his *vaadan,* which became a new *shaily*.

Twentieth Century (June 16, 1895 to 1927)—Ustaad Inayat Khan
Menfred Junious wrote in his book, *The Sitar:* "This great artist introduced thumri flavor in sitar."

Sir Bimal Kant
This artist put his best efforts into popularizing the sitar.

Twentieth Century (1926)—Ustaad Vilayat Khan
He reduced the number of strings of sitar from seven to six and put *gayaki ang* in his *vaadan*, which became very popular and people found it easy to learn.

Twentieth Century (1881–1972)—Ustaad Alaudin Khan
The great musician put his best efforts into his art. He was a perfect sitarist. Ustaad Alaudin Khan Sahib put *been ang* in his recitals to make

them more beautiful. He taught sitar to Pt. Ravi Shankar ji, sarod to Ustaad Ali Akbar, and surbahar to his daughter Annapurna.

Ustaad Ali Akbar Khan

Being the son of a great Ustaad Alaudin Khan, he had all the talents of his genius father. He made this instrument popular, not only among Indians, but in foreign countries also.

April 7, 1920—Pt. Ravi Shankar ji

This great artist has made our country proud of him. Even at the age of 92, he is a regular sitar player. He plays been *ang*, sarod technique, and *gayaki ang* in his *vaadan*. He has produced the chirping of birds, the burst of clouds, the sounds of a waterfall, dancing tunes, and what not. In his orchestra, he has played sitar *tukras* for filling the gap and has beautified the orchestration with sitar playing.

(1927)—Abdul Haleem Zafar Khan Sahib

He made Zaafar Khani *guts*.

There have been many great musican artists in the twentieth century, such as Shujjat Hussain Khan, Arvind Parikh, and Buddhaditaya Mukerjee, who all are trying their best to enrich the sitar *vaadan* with their own techniques.

CHAPTER 5

Sitar *Gharanas*

The Meaning of *Gharana*

In the Bengali language, the word "*Gharana*" means "born of" or belonging to or relating to a family.

The word "*Ghar*" means *guni-bangsha prampara*. This last word means the regular line of succession of family tradition that has skill in music.

Some take "*Gharana*" to be a Hindi word meaning "family," in the broad sense of the word. But when we talk about music *Gharanas*, we mean the "*Prampara*" of one family. The *Prampara* includes:

- Continuity for generations
- Particular location links
- Individual style
- Musicians enrich the tradition with new efforts

We see it takes a long time to become a *Gharana*. In order to come into existence, the same style of music must be maintained by the family of musicians for at least three generations.

The Origin of *Gharana*

Indian music has made a long journey. It has seen the best and the worst times. It has been appreciated at one place by some and disliked at another place by the others. Whichever style it might have adopted, there were gurus and *shishyas* to teach and learn.

Gharana means Guru *Shishya Prampara*. This word has been in use for a long period. *Gharana* has had different words used for it:

- Branch
- School
- *Geeti*
- *Vaani*
- *Mat*

Shiv-mat and *Brahm mat* were the great traditional institutions of dance.

Existence of a Gharana

Every *Gharana* has its own traditions and techniques, which are continued from generation to generation, and every technique is referred to as *vaadan shaily*. In each *Gharana*, there are some specific ragas and *Bandishen*, which make it famous for their *Baaj* or *Chal*.

In sitar *Gharanas*, every artist has his own style or *baaj* or *vaadan shaily* or *vidhi*. These *shailies* were called *Gharanas*. The specific *gayan, vaadan,* or *nritya shailies* had their own *Gharanas* named after the vocalists, instrumentalists, and dancers.

These *Gharanas* have been keeping our art alive, and we are lucky enough to have the traditional music with us. Vocal classical music had great effect on sitar *Gharanas*. The sitar *vaadan shaily* was started from the base of vocal music. From the very beginning of the fourteenth century, classical vocal music played a great role in the invention of new styles in instrumental music. It has gone through so many hands that new techniques and *baaj vidhies* came into existence. So *Gharana* is a compound of a social feature (the membership) and a cultural one (musical style). *Gharana* is a family tradition, and a lineage of hereditary musicians, their disciples, and the particular musical style they represent.

Historically, musical families became *Gharanas* as a result of patronage. They are the real custodians of the cultural heritage of Indian music. In this role, they have not only preserved our traditional music in its original beauty and glory, but they also have enriched it with artistry. A *Gharana* usually consists of a line of hereditary musicians who are referred to as the *Khandaan*. Their style of music is also known as *Khandaani cheez.*

The *Khandaan* forms an inner circle that may include special *gats, toraas,* and techniques. In the *Khandaan* tradition, the owner gives the lessons to a favorite disciple only or to his family members.

The particular aesthetic, which shows the *bol* with *laya,* is the foundation of several systems of sitar *baaj.* The ancient Sanskrit texts formulated rules, which were later adopted by other musicians. There were four principal schools of music according to references in the classical period (600–500 BC). They were called *Sampardayas.* Here may be detected the origin of *Gharanas* of the present century.

The next phase of development was reached with the emergence of *Geetis,* that is, songs rendered in different *vaanis.* Then these *vaanis* or *geetis* gradually assimilated into *Dhrupad, Khayal,* and instrumental music. These *vaanis* then were employed by the *beenkaars,* which are used even today.

At the time, *khayal* was gaining ascendancy, new trends developed in sitar playing. *Khayal* made its impact on sitar *vaadan.* Maseet Khan, a direct descendant of Tansen, adopted the sitar to the *Dhrupad* tradition. Later, Raheemsen and Amritsen further developed this technique. But it was Imdad Khan who added some sympathetic strings and made this instrument richer in tone and fuller in sound. The use of embellishments became liberal, and Inayat Khan made further innovations and gave a new direction in playing sitar. Thus, the ancient musical tradition has undergone many changes. The tradition of *Vaanis* and *Geetis*—as also the Guru *Shishya Prampara* or the master-disciple tradition—formed the basis of music *Gharanas* in India.

Changing *Vaadan Shailies* of Different *Gharanas* of Sitar

With the establishment of Muslim rule in North India, Indian music developed quickly in a new direction, although there was not a complete rupture with the tradition inherited from the past.

Fourteenth Century—Music gained popularity during the fourteenth century. Many ragas and instruments were invented, and the sitar is listed in one of those instruments.

Eighteenth Century—During the reign of Muhammad Shah Rangeeley (1719–1748), music received extensive patronage. There are several versions and opinions regarding different styles of sitar playing during this period, but it would be commonly accepted that *gats* or *Bandish* on the sitar crystalized during the later half of the eighteenth century. It may be significant to mention that at this stage, the followers of Tansen were divided into two main streams—one of Beenkaars and the other of Rababiyas. The Beenkaars gave importance to *Swara* presentation, while the Rababiyas laid stress on *Laya* in their presentations.

The sitar absorbed the use of both *Swara* and *Laya*, no doubt based on the *Dhrupad* style of vocal music. This was the era when Maseet Khani *gats* in *vilambit teen talas* were played on the sitar. Tracing further development of *gats*, we come across the names of Raheemsen, who developed the sitar into a versatile and highly effective instrument during the eighteenth century. *Dhrupad ang* was used. Apart from *gats* in *teen taal*, several *gats* were composed in *Jhaptal* as well. Small *meends* were also performed. Maseet Khani *baaj* was being developed principally in Delhi, Jaipur, and Alwar, whereas another style known as Raza Khani *baaj* was gaining popularity and was being developed in Lucknow, Kashi, and Jaunpur. Raza Khan, actually one of the principal students of Maseet Khan, developed this style in sitar *vaadan*.

While the Maseet Khani *baaj* has a certain amount of dignity and depth, the Raza Khani style has a unique beauty of *Laykaari*.

Important Maseet Khani *gat* players were Bahadur Khan, son of Maseet Khan, Ustad Dulhe Khan of Jaipur, Gulam Hussain Khan of Delhi, and Pan Khan of Mathura.

The famous Raza Khani *gat* players of that period were Gulam Raza Khan, Panna Lal Vijpayi, Babu Ishwari Prasad, Barkat Ali Khan, and Gulam Mohammed.

Firoj Khani was another style which flourished, but it was overpowered by Maseet Khani and Raza Khani *gats*. The Firoj Khani *gats* started from the ninth *matra*, first line (*Sthai*), and ended on a note of middle octave and the second line started from the same note.

Nineteenth Century—It would be no exaggeration to say that this period was the golden period for popularity of sitar. The stylistic evolution of the sitar reached great heights in this period. Amrit Sen, a famous sitarist, introduced a technique of *gat-toraa*, and the use of *Tihai* was introduced in this period by the great sitar Maestro Ustaad Inayat Khan. Ustaad Imdad Khan and Ustaad Barkatulla Khan introduced *Jhala* technique in sitar *vaadan*. The use of both hands was equal. The left hand started creating melody and gradually started being more active with the more *swaras* and more *mizraab* strokes.

A complete performance of the sitar included *Alaap, Jor-alaap, gats* (slow and fast *gat*), *toraas* of both *gats,* and then finally the *Jhala*. Centers like Jaipur, Delhi, Gwalior, Alwar, Rewa, Baroda, Jaunpur, Lucknow, and Rampur became the focal points of sitar playing.

Twentieth Century—Many of the rulers had their own musical courts and they themselves were sometimes good musicians. These courts preserved and developed within the *Gharanas* of North India, Lucknow, Jaunpur, and Gwalior.

Generally, a sitarist learns a *baaj* and then uses it to interpret the music that he or she has learnt from a *Gharana* artist. It indicates a particular *Gharana* of which the *baaj* is from.

The famous sitar *Gharanas* and *shailies*, which have been prevalent in India, are as follows:

Gwalior *Gharana*—Gulam Ali Khan (Haddu Khan's Sarod *shaily*)
Jaipur *Gharana*—Tansen's Senia *Gharana* (Sen Vanshiya *shaily*)
Vishnupur *Gharana*—Mixed *vaadan shaily*
Indore *Gharana*—Mixed *vaadan shaily* of Ustaad Babu Khan
Etawa *Gharana*—Imdad Khani Shaily.
Maihar—Rampur *Gharana*, Ustaad Alaudin Khan's *shaily*

1. Gwalior Gharana—Haddu Khan started this *Gharana*. Wahid Khan, Maraad Khan, Gulaam Khan, Lalit Khan, Rais Khan, and Abdul Haleem

Zaafar Khan come from this lineage. These Ustaads never made notations, and hence we are deprived of their precious music. They gave lessons to few of their disciples.

2. Jaipur Sitar Gharana or Senia Gharana—The city of Jaipur was founded in seventeenth century. In the year 1739, Senia musicians left Delhi because the Darbaar of Mohammed Shah fell, and they sought the patronage of Rajput courts in Jaipur. These musicians were descendants of Senia Beenkaar Maseet Khan, who according to the history of Indian music, developed the first classical sitar *baaj*. Maseet Khan's great-grandson, Raheemsen, developed *Dhrupad shaily*, which had been started by Tansen. Maseet Khan was the first to give the instrument the status of a mature, classical, solo instrument. Senia *Gharana* introduced the following rules and made some of the changes:

- Maseet Khan made Maseet Khani *gat* in *vilambit laya*. (A *gat* is a short musical form consisting of a rhythmical pattern based on the strokes of *mizraab*.)
- Raza Khan made Raza Khani *gats* or Drut *gats*, which were made beautiful with *taraas* and *Jhala*.
- Sukh Chain was perfect in *Alaap Chuuri*. He played the *alaap*, *Jhala* on sitar for hours and hours together with *meend* work.
- Raheemsen added *Beenkari ang* in sitar *vaadan*.
- Amrit Sen played the same technique, sitar *vaadan*, and with the help of his father, he started playing *khayal-ang-in* sitar.
- Nihalsen was another sitarist in Senia *Gharana*, who started the *tarb* string work on sitar.

There have been many artists in Senia *Gharana*, who continued to develop this art of music. Ustad Ameer Khan, Ustad Barktullah Khan, Ustad Imdad Khan, Ashiq Ali Khan, and Mushtak Ali Khan are the famous ones.

The Sen Vanshiya artists are strict enough not to play any other *Gharana*'s *Bandishes*. They believe in the sweet melody of the raga. Amrit Sen had his favorite disciples: Nihalsen, Ameer Khan, and Ustaad Imdad Khan. Imdad Khan started his own *Gharana*. The Jaipur Sitar *baaj* is depicted in Debu Chaudhary's book *The Sitar and Its Techniques*. The *meend* work is given much more importance in this *baaj*.

3. Imdad Khani Gharana—His father, Sahebdad Khan, was a great sitarist. Imdad Khan followed his father's footsteps by developing the *meend, ghaseet,* and *jhala* work in sitar. Imdad Khan's son, Inayat Khan, and Vaheed Khan made the *gats, jor alaap,* and then the *gats* were played with *toraas.* His disciple, Vilayat Khan, continued this *shaily.* Vilayat Khan's *vaadan* includes strong *mizraab* strokes and difficult *toraas.* Imdad Khan lived in Calcutta for about twenty years where he continued his *riyaaz* of the sitar. Arvind Parikh, Ustaad Alaudin Khan's disciple, was a great sitarist.

From this very *Gharana,* the great sitar players, Shujat Khan and Nishaat Khan, are continuing the work. The other great sitarist from Imdad Khani *Gharana* is Budhaditya Mukherjee from Bhilai. Both Shujaat Khan and Budhaditya Mukherjee play *gayaki ang* on the sitar. Shujaat Hussain Khan's *vaadan shaily* has sweetness of sound. He sings while playing on the sitar. He plays *spaat taans* with great perfection. His *Jhala* work is so beautiful, even in the fastest speed. He has such control over *swaras, laya,* and *Taal* that the audience remains spellbound. When interviewed at Rose Garden, Kala Bhawan, Sector 16, Chandigarh, he said that he likes to play *gayaki ang* more.

Budhaditya Mukerjee learned the sitar from his father, and his *vaadan shaily* has also the *gayaki* and *tantarkari* in it. When interviewed, he told me that he belongs to the Imdad Khani *Gharana* and has adopted that *shaily.* Even then, he had his own inventions also, to which he keeps adding. He likes fast tempo *gats.* He is at his best with *meend* work in *alaap.* He stressed in the interview that he has learned from his father, who is from Imdadi *Gharana,* and in this *vaadan shaily* there is a mixture of *Tantakari* and *gayaki ang.*

4. Alaudin Khan's Rampur Gharana—The late Alaudin Khan took lessons from Muhammad Vajeer Khan of Tansen's Vansh. His son, Ustaad Ali Akbar Khan, became a famous sarodist. He taught his *vaadan shaily* to Pt. Ravi Shankar, who is his son-in-law and is at the height of fame. Pt. Ravi Shankar's sitar *vaadan shaily* has the qualities that can depict every human emotion, seasonal effects, birds chirping, the flow of the rivers, the roar of the sea, and clouds through the power of his fingers. He popularized *Dhuns* on the sitar, based on folk melodies. He has made this instrument a must in almost every song.

Kramatulla Khan is another great sitarist who took his music education from his father, Nayamatulla Khan. Nayamatulla Khan was a sarodist, but his son mixed the sarod *vaadan* with the sitar, and it became a new *vaadan shaily,* which gave birth to a new technique. Now the artist does not have any compulsion as to which *Gharana* he should adopt. He can mix more than one *gharanedaar gats* and *toraas,* and a new style emerges.

5. Indore Gharana—This famous *Gharana* was founded by Ustaad Babu Khan. Bhagwat Saran Shama wrote in *Sitar Malika*: "Abdul Haleem Zafar, born in 1927 in Jawra, is also from the same *Gharana*. He uses *kan swara* in his sitar *vaadan* with great perfection. The other techniques remain the same as other artists use. He gives free sitar *vaadan* in film sangeet."

The *Gharanas* can be kept alive only by hardworking artists who become professionals. The *Gharana* is an institution that, over the past 400 years, has acted as the custodian of the heritage of North Indian classical music. These schools exhibit a strong degree of stylistic homogeneity vis-à-vis *baaj* and *chaal*.

Nowadays, only two types of *gats*/Bandish compositions of sitar are prevalent, namely Maseet Khani and Raza Khani.

The Maseet Khani *gat* invariably uses the following set of *bols*:

x				2				0				3			
1	2	3	4	5	6	7	8	9	10	11	12	13	14	15	16
											SaSa Dir	Re Da	GaGa Dir	Ma Da	Pa Ra
Dha Da	Ni Da	Sa Ra	SaSa Dir	Ni Da	DhaDha Dir	Pa Da	Ma Ra	Ga Da	Re Da	Sa Ra					
											SaSaSa DaDir	Re Da	GaGaGa DaDir	Ma Da	Pa Ra
Dha Da	Ni Da	Sa Ra	SaSaSa DaDir	Ni Da	DhaDha DaDir	Pa Da	Ma Ra	Ga Da	Re Da	Sa Ra					

Sharmistha Sen writes in *String Instruments of North India*

Gats of different shailies in different beats

Raga Gujari Todi of Amrit Sen

	x				2				0				3			
	1	2	3	4	5	6	7	8	9	10	11	12	13	14	15	16
Sthai												DhaDha	Sa	NiDha	MaGaGa	MaMa
												DaDir	Da	DaDir	DaDir	DaRa
	Dha	Ni	Sa	SaSa	Ni	DhaDha	Ma	Dha	ReGa	Re	Sa					
	Da	Da	Ra	Dir	Da	Dir	Da	Ra	DaRa	Da	Ra					
Antra												SaRe	SaRe	ReRe	Sa	Sa
												Dir	Dir	Dir	Da	Ra
	Dha	NiNi	Sa	SaSa	Re	GaGa	Ma	Dha	MaDhaDha	MaGa	Re					
	Da	Dir	Da	Dir	Da	Dir	Da	Ra	DaDir	DaDa	Ra					

Maseet Khani Gat in teen taal -16 beats 4+4+4+4
Raga Vilas Khani Todi

	x				2				0				3			
	1	2	3	4	5	6	7	8	9	10	11	12	13	14	15	16
Sthai												SaRe	Ni	SaSa	Ga	Ma
												Dir	Da	Dir	Da	Ra
	Pa	Dha	Pa	MaMa	Ga	MaMa	Pa	Ma	Ga	Re	Sa					
	Da	Da	Ra	Dir	Da	Dir	Da	Ra	Da	Da	Ra					
												NiNi	Da	NiNi	Sa	Sa
												Dir	Da	Dir	Da	Ra
	Ga	Re	Sa	MaMa	Ga	MaMa	Pa	Ma	Ga	Re	Sa					
	Da	Da	Ra	Dir	Da	Dir	Da	Ra	Da	Da	Ra					
Antra												MaMa	Ga	MaMa	Dha	Ni
												Dir	Da	Dir	Da	Ra
	Sa	Re	Sa	SaSa	Ni	SaSa	Re	Sa	Ni	Dha	Pa					
	Da	Da	Ra	Dir	Da	Dir	Da	Ra	Da	Da	Ra					
												GaGa	Re	SaSa	Ni	Dha
												Dir	Da	Dir	Da	Ra
	Ni	Dha	Pa	MaMa	Ga	MaMa	Pa	Ma	Ga	Re	Sa					
	Da	Da	Ra	Dir	Da	Dir	Da	Ra	Da	Da	Ra					

Sharmistha Sen writes in *String Instruments of North India*

Raga Desh: Ustad Imdad Khan Sahib

	x			0			
1	2	3	4	5	6	7	8

Sthai

1	2	3	4	5	6	7	8
Sa	ReRe	Re	Ma	_	Pa	Ma	Pa
Da	Dir	Da	Ra	_	Da	Da	Ra
Ni	Ni	Sa	Ni	Sa	ReRe	Sa	Ni
Da	Da	Ra	Da	Da	Dir	Da	Ra
Dha	Pa	DhaPa	PaPa	Ma	MaMa	Ga	Re
Dir	Da	Dir	Dir	Da	Dir	Da	Ra
Re	NiNi	Dha	Ni	Dha	Ni	Pa	Dha
Da	Dir	Da	Ra	Da	Da	Ra	Da
Ma	Pa	DhaDha	PaPa	Ma	MaGa	_Ga	Re_
Da	Ra	Dir	Dir	Da	RDa	R	Da_
Re	PaPa	Pa	Ma	Ga	Re	Ga	Ga
Da	Dir	Da	Ra	Da	Da	Ra	Da

Antra

1	2	3	4	5	6	7	8
Ma	Ma	Pa	Pa	PaNi	Pa	Ni	Ni
Da	Da	Ra	Da	Dir	Da	Da	Ra
Sa	Sa	NiNi	SaSa	Re	ReNi	Ni	Sa
Da	Ra	Dir	Dir	Da	Dir	Da	Ra
Sa	GaGa	Re	Ma	_	Ga	Re	Sa
Da	Dir	Da	Ra	_	Da	Da	Ra
Ni	Sa	ReRe	SaSa	Ni	NiDha	_Dha	Pa
Da	Ra	Dir	Dir	Da	RDa	_R	Da_
Pa	ReRe	Sa	Re	_	Re	Sa	ReRe
Da	Dir	Da	Ra	_	Da	Da	Dir
Sa	Re	_	Re	Re	_	Re	_
Da	Ra	_	Da	Da	_	Ra	_
Re	PaPa	Pa	Ma	Ga	Re	Ga	Ga
Da	Dir	Da	Ra	Da	Ra	Da	Ra

Raza Khani *gat* In Raga Bhupali Teen-Taal—16 Beats 4+4+4+4

	x				2				0				3			
	1	2	3	4	5	6	7	8	9	10	11	12	13	14	15	16
Sthai									Sa	ReRe	Ga	Re	Sa	DhaDha	Sa	Re
									Da	Dir	Da	Ra	Da	Dir	Da	Ra
	Ga	_	Ga	Re	Ga	PaPa	Dha	Pa								
	Da	_	Da	Ra	Da	Dir	Da	Ra								
									Re	ReRe	Ga	Ga	Pa	PaPa	Dha	Pa
									Da	Dir	Da	Ra	Da	Dir	Da	Ra
	Sa	DhaDha	Pa	Pa	Ga	GaRe	_Re	Sa								
	Da	Dir	Da	Ra	Da	RDa	_R	Da_								
Antra									Ga	GaGa	Pa	Dha	Sa	_	Sa	Sa
									Da	Dir	Da	Ra	Da	_	Da	Ra
	Sa	ReRe	Ga	Re	Sa	ReRe	Sa	Sa								
	Da	Dir	Da	Ra	Da	Dir	Da	Ra								
									Ga	ReRe	Sa	Dha	Re	SaSa	Dha	Pa
									Da	Dir	Da	Ra	Da	Dir	Da	Ra
	Ga	PaPa	DhaDha	PaPa	Ga	GaRe	_Re	Sa								
	Da	Dir	Dir	Dir	Da	RDa	_R	Da_								

Raza Khani (Raga Vilakhani Todi) in different beats
Ek-Taal 12 beats - 2+2+2+2+2+2
Re Ga Dha Ni Komal Swaras

	x		0		2		0		3		4	
	1	2	3	4	5	6	7	8	9	10	11	12
Sthai	Ga	GaGa	Re	Re	Sa	Sa	Re	ReRe	Ni	NIDha	Dha	Sa
	Da	Dir	Da	Ra	Da	Ra	Da	Dir	Da	Dir	Da	Ra
Antra	Dha	DhaDha	Ma	MaMa	Ga	Ga	Pa	PaPa	Dha	DhaDha	Sa	Sa
	Da	Dir	Da	Dir	Da	Ra	Da	Dir	Da	Dir	Da	Ra
	Re	ReRe	Ni	NiNi	Dha	Pa	Ma	MaMa	Ga	ReRe	Sa	Sa
	Da	Dir	Da	Dir	Da	Ra	Da	Dir	Da	Dir	Da	Ra

Raza Khani Gat - Raga Vilaskhani Todi—Taal Kehrawa - 8 Beats - 4+4

	x				0			
	1	2	3	4	5	6	7	8
Sthai								
	Ga	ReRe	Sa	Sa	Ni	DhaDha	Sa	Sa
	Da	Dir	Da	Ra	Da	Dir	Da	Ra
	Re	GaGa	*Ma*	*Ma*	Ga	ReRe	Sa	*Sa*
	Da	Dir	*Da*	*Ra*	Da	Dir	Da	*Ra*
Antra								
	Dha	*MaMa*	Ga	Ga	Pa	DhaDha	Sa	Sa
	Da	*Dir*	Da	*Ra*	Da	Dir	Da	Ra
	Re	*GaGa*	*Ra*	*Ma*	Ni	DhaDha	Sa	Sa
	Da	*Dir*	*Da*	*Ra*	Da	Dir	Da	Ra
	Re	*NiNi*	*Dha*	*Dha*	Pa	DhaDha	Ma	Ma
	Da	*Dir*	*Da*	*Ra*	Da	Dir	Da	Ra
	Ga	*ReRe*	Sa	Sa	Ni	DhaDha	Sa	Sa
	Da	*Dir*	Da	Ra	Da	Dir	Da	Ra

Raga-Vilaskhani Todi
Raza Khani Gat in Taal-Rupak - 7 beats 3+2+2

	x			2		3	
	1	2	3	4	5	6	7
Sthai	Ga	ReRe	Ni	Dha	DhaDha	Sa	Sa
	Da	Dir	Da	Da	Dir	Da	Ra
	Re	GaGa	Ma	Ga	ReRe	Sa	Sa
	Da	Dir	Da	Da	Dir	Da	Ra
Antra	Dha	MaMa	Ga	Pa	DhaDha	Sa	Sa
	Da	Dir	Da	Da	Dir	Da	Ra
	Re	GaGa	Re	Ni	DhaDha	Sa	Sa
	Da	Dir	Da	Da	Dir	Da	Ra
	Re	NiNi	Dha	Pa	DhaDha	Ma	Ma
	Da	Dir	Da	Da	Dir	Da	Ra
	Ga	ReRe	Ni	Dha	DhaDha	Sa	Sa
	Da	Dir	Da	Da	Dir	Da	Ra

Raga-Vilaskhani Todi
Raza Khani Gat in Taal-Dadra - 6 beats 3+3

	x			0		
	1	2	3	4	5	6
Sthai	Ga	ReRe	Ni	Dha	DhaDha	Sa
	Da	Dir	Da	Da	Dir	Da
	Dha	MaMa	Ga	Pa	DhaDha	Sa
	Da	Dir	Da	Da	Dir	Da
Antra	Re	GaGa	Re	Ni	DhaDha	Sa
	Da	Dir	Da	Da	Dir	Da
	Re	NiNi	Dha	Pa	DhaDha	Ma
	Da	Dir	Da	Da	Dir	Da
	Ga	ReRe	Ni	Dha	DhaDha	Sa
	Da	Dir	Da	Da	Dir	Da

We see that during the twentieth century, or the present period, sitar *vaadan shailies* have achieved a lot, and as change is the law of nature, *vaadan shailies* of the sitar have gone through vast changes. *Dhrupad*-based compositions of earlier periods are gradually being replaced by *Khayal*-based compositions. Both Maseet Khani and Raza Khani *gats* have undergone quite some changes:

- The *laya* of Maseet Khani *gat* has been increased. It is played just like slow-tempo *khayal* singing is done.
- In the modern period, in Raza Khani *gats*, the use of the *bols* is almost nonexistent as most of the *gats* are based on *khayal Bandish* and are presented in the *gayaki ang* style.
- The use of the left hand has increased considerably along with the right-hand movements. *Meend*, Kan *Swara*, Murki, Khatka, *gamak*, *Krintan*, *zamzama*, and more are extensively used in the development of the *gats*.
- *Alaap* has gained the height of popularity. Before the first half of the twentieth century, it was given importance, but not much time was given to *swara vistuar*. But after 1950, the *alaap* has become the main part of sitar *vaadan*, which introduces the raga to the audience and depicts its emotions and feelings. Along with the melodic and rhythmic development, *alaap* has achieved great relative importance. Before 1950, the *gats* were thought to be the pivot around which the music presentation moved, in the context of a short *alaap*, *taans* or *toraas* with *tihais* with the beat of tabla and lastly the *Jhala*. *Alaap* has reduced the relative importance and the primary role of *gats*.
- The *bols* of *mizraab*, starting with the *gat*, and structure of formation of *vilambit* and *drut gats* do not follow hard and fast rules.

Although rhythm is the base of all music, *khayal gayaki* has affected the Indian sitar *vaadan shaily* so much that the artist is free to play anything in any style at any time and to any limit of time. In earlier times—up to the middle of the nineteenth century—*gats* had the pivotal role in sitar performances. They had the unique beauty of rhythm and emotions. There are sitar players who can perform the *gat vaadan* for long periods, but then the repetition of *tihais* after every *toraa*, spoils the beauty of the raga. *Vaadan shailies* of the sitar have been going through many changes with the developed techniques of beautifying the performance, and this process will continue with the change of artists and with the change of time.

Pt. Gopal Krishan ji, a distinguished *Vichitra* Veena player, told me in an interview at P. U. Chandigarh that he has adopted some of the techniques of the sitar in his *vaadan,* and the sitar has adopted veena *vaadan shaily* in many ways. He learned this art from his father, Pt. Nand Kishore ji. Gopal ji said that *alaap* of sitar has been taken from vichitra veena.

In 1977, I was invited to attend a seminar on Sangeet Ate Usda Gurbaani Te Parbhav, in Central State Library, Sector 17, Chandigarh, which was arranged by Dr. Sr. Nirender Singh Virdi of Jallandhar. I had a chance to ask many questions about the sitar which was my subject of teaching. He told me that sitar has adopted the *alaap* of the veena and it is the child of the veena (*Tri-tantri* veena). *Vichitra* veena is the developed *roop* of t*ritantri* veena. Slow *gats* look graceful on veena, whereas the sitar shines in both *vilambit* and *drut gats.* In modern sitar, *vaadan shailies, gayaki-ang,* and *Tantri-ang* have taken a great place. The credit for this type of *vaadan shaily* goes to Imdad Khan and Vilayat Khan. They have brought the sitar very close to the human voice.

Budhaditya Mukerjee, when interviewed at Bhartiya Vidya Bhawan in October 1995, at Sector 27, Chandigarh, told me that the sitar has vast techniques to be learned. Vilayat Khan Sahib's style of *jor* has been adopted by the young artists. Nowadays, *khayals* are played on the sitar and heard by audiences with great pleasure.

Pt. Ravi Shankar ji is the most celebrated musician of our country today. He has enriched the sitar by introducing the *vaadan shailies* of vocal music and other instruments, such as the sarod. He has made many ragas with mishrit *swaras;* that is, he mixed two to three ragas and then originated one new raga. He has mastery over every *tala.*

Nikhil Banerji has contributed a lot in the field of sitar *vaadan.* He has given *gats* that are woven with *Khayal gayaki ang.*

Another noted sitar player, Muushtaq Ali Khan, bases his compositions on Maseet Khani and Raza Khani styles. He maintains the purity of the tradition and plays the *gats* always in *Teentaal* because he is a firm believer in the old tradition of *mizraab bols.* He prefers to play the raga in *Dhrupad Ang.* He renders the raga in veena technique. For example, his compositions include *Alaap*, *Vilambit gat*, and *Madhya gat,* which includes all the sitar techniques and the fourth stage, *Drut gat,* and then *Jhala.*

Toward the end of the eighteenth century, Ustaad Imdad Khan made revolutionary changes in the sitar *vaadan shaily* by introducing new techniques. He made some new *bols* of *mizraab*, which were used while playing *gayaki ang* on sitar. Pt. Ravi Shankar ji started playing both *alaap* and *gat toraas* on sitar. Previously the *alaap* was played on the *sur-bahar*. New experiments will introduce more techniques and more new innovative *vaadan shailies* will be produced by the great artists.

CHAPTER 6

The Sitar in
Indian Classical Music

M any artists in the nineteenth century devoted their whole lives to the promotion of classical music, but even after so many efforts, classical music could not reach the expected heights.

After independence, Indian classical music has not yet been able to regain the status it had in the past in the Indian society. It is not as common and popular as light or folk music. The changing attitudes and atmosphere of the new generation and the lack of devotional teachers in the field of classical music are responsible for this situation.

If we consider the period from Tansen to Sadarang, more than two hundred years ago, we conclude that the *Dhrupad shaily* was predominant, so the sitar players also adopted the same technique. *Alaap* was prominent. Further, considering the period from Sadarang to Fayyaz Khan, almost two hundred years, *Dhrupad* was the main *vaadan shaily* in sitar playing, but on the other side simultaneously Tappa and Thumri made the classical music slightly easier to learn. Light music started gaining popularity.

The first and the foremost reason for the downfall of the classical music was the lack of practice or *Sadhna* and devotion of the teacher toward classical music. The artists performed just for money and fame.

Pt. Vishnu Digamber Pulaskar made best efforts to eradicate all the defects in music system and to some extent he was successful. This work of Pulaskar was taken over by Pt. Vishnu Narayan Bhatkhande, who took great pains to make improvements in the music system. The greatest thing he did was the invention of a new system named "Notation System." He made collections of all the old *gats* after meeting the Ustaads of that period and wrote down the notations of all the *bandishes* and *cheesen* of olden times. It made the Indian music easy, because even in the absence of the guru, the *shishya* could practice the raga by reading and studying the *swara lipi* of any raga, or *Khayal.* The period after Bhatkhande can be referred to as the worst-effected period or dark period for Indian classical music.

Popularization of the Sitar

There was a sudden change in the interests of the people in classical music, and as a result, light music took the place of classical music. Due to the struggle for independence, disturbances, and political imbalance in the country, all the great artists had a setback. Film music attracted more people when the Bhatkhande notation system came into existence. It was easy to teach, and there were many books published that included all the ragas or *khayals* sung or played by different *ustaads*. Classical music was limited only to vocalists. There was lack of instrumentalists, although there were a few sarod and veena *vaaduks.* The sitar started to take a place in performance. The gurus started giving lessons in sitar playing to some of the selected *shishyas.*

All India Radio gave the opportunity to the sitarists to perform. It started paying them good money. The government started giving economic help to the artists so that they could develop their art and talent easily and to their own taste and for the common public. The audience started taking interest in classical instrumental music again.

The Sangeet Natak academy made great efforts to promote classical instrumental music. It has produced a great number of artists in instrumental as well as vocal music. The artists from Gwalior *Gharana* and Senia *Gharana* have done a lot for the advancement of the unique artistic place of the sitar in Indian classical music.

Akaash Vaani relays the regular programmers of Indian classical instrumental music. The schools and colleges organize the competitions for classical instrumental music, which promote the love for music among the students.

Appreciation of the Sitar

The sitar is the most popular and sophisticated instrument that has acquired a great place in the Indian classical music. It is played in almost every song, *bhajan, ghazal,* solo performance, orchestra, and in folk tunes. The sitar is used in playback music, which includes classical ragas.

The artists like Pt. Ravi Shankar ji, Ustaad Alaudin Khan, Ustaad Vilayat Khan, Shujaat Hussain Khan, Nishaat Hussain Khan, Kartik Kumar, Shahid Parvez, Shameem Ahmad, the late Nikhil Benerjee, Debu Chaudhary, Mani Lal Naag, and others have played vital roles in the promotion and development of sitar in Indian classical music.

Now the sitar enjoys a great place in Indian classical music, and it is present at almost every public function. It has the capacity to produce the nine *rasas* of Indian culture, and it can play Western tunes as well. Westerners are learning this *saaz* with devotion. It has an individuality in group performances. It is played in light music, orchestra, and devotional songs with a classical tinge.

The sitar can produce flat notes, which no other instrument has been able to do. The classical sitar *vaadan* has the spiritual effect upon human mind. The resonant sounds, which the strings of the sitar produce, can heal the old diseases in a few minutes if produced rightly and properly.

The sitar in Indian classical music shows its perfection in *Alaap,* which can be played on the sitar for hours and hours. The classical ragas include the following pieces, which are one above the other in beauty, rhythm, and aesthetic:

- *Alaap*
- Jor-*alaap*
- *Jhala* (small)
- Vilambit *Gat*
- *Toraas*
- *Raza Khani Gat*
- *Toraas*
- *Jhala.*

The vibrations of the sitar make us forget every tension, and we are lost in a world of peace and happiness. Many of the great artists of India have settled in other countries, and the others continue to go abroad because they feel that the Indian government is not rewarding them well. It is a pity that we are deprived of the treasures of the big *ustaads* of our country when they leave their own country and settle abroad.

The sitar has received appreciation in Western countries in classical programs where Pt. Ravi Shankar ji gave performances with Yehudi Menuhin, who was an Indian settled abroad and a great musician.

There is nothing in the Indian system that would prevent a natural development in that direction, provided that the impulses spring not from intellectual curiosity but from inner necessity. The musicians of modern period have developed this art so much with their ingenuity and imagination in composing the ragas that the sitar has achieved wonderful results in enriching Indian classical music. New techniques are being developed in Indian classical music. The sitar has a high place in every function, and it always starts with the sitar's classical tone. This instrument has created taste and interest in Indian classical music.

Now, the people feel an artistic sense in this instrument, when classical ragas are performed on the sitar. The music-minded appreciate its *vaadan,* and the common man enjoys the classical music on the sitar, because the classical *swaras* of the sitar work as medicine for the sick and are powerful curers.

The sitar was used as an accompanying instrument in the initial period, but as veena became an independent solo instrument, the sitar naturally followed similar development. The sitar was used just as a pause filler to maintain *Nayas* notes on which the vocalist made a pause. This instrument had its own potentialities as a solo instrument. It has the sweet melody. The crystallization of sitar *gats* has won the hearts of people.

During the twentieth century, the stylistic evolution of sitar reached greater heights, and it is hoped that it will open vast fields for its popularity in Indian classical music. The twentieth century can be said to be the golden period for the sitar's rise and success. The Indian classical music on sitar has achieved completely new dimensions. The changes are fairly radical. The sitar *vaadan* has become intellectual and imaginative. It is an instrument that expresses the feelings and emotions of one's heart. The composite improvisation of classical *vaadan* of the sitar has reached the zenith during the present period.

Now the enriched *gat* style of the sitar, with melodic and rhythmic development, has reached its height. The *alaap* form has achieved greatest relative importance. The whole *vaadan* is done as *Alaap*. Previously the *gat* was the heartbeat but now *Alaap* is the heartbeat of sitar performances. The garland of Indian classical music has become more beautiful with this instrument. During Pt. Ravi Shankar ji's extensive tours of Western countries, sitar concerts in Raga *Darbari Kanhra, Marwa,* and *Bageshwari* with *Dhrupad* styles were accepted by the audience with great enthusiasm. Dedicated experiments and consistent research have brought new influences in traditional style of Indian classical music. According to Pt. Ravi Shankar ji, the pure artist must be free to choose his style of playing. Yehudi Menuhin said in an interview on Delhi TV that Indian classical music is innocent, which binds the audience and the performer alike, and Pt. ji's sitar has the power of doing this miracle.

The young artists are doing their best to make sitar in classical music popular.

Indian music has unlimited potential for development. Music with its notes forms, emotions, expressions, and highly developed science, conveys deeper meaning of human struggle, happiness, joy, and a variety of moods. Given the proper scope, understanding, and opportunities for development, with active support from private as well as public sectors, it can blossom into an extraordinary medium of expression with its infinite scope for variety and progress based on materials accumulating through the centuries. With its classical aspect and folk music, the sitar has woven into our compositions a world of human emotions, mental, and spiritual experience.

Renowned and Flourishing Sitarists

Here are the viewpoints of some of the sitarists interviewed.

- **Pandit Uma Shankar Mishra's Sitar Recital** (Kamni Auditorium, Delhi, March 7, 1993, International Festival of Music held at Delhi)—He mobilized a marvelous *Alaap* stretch, developing the raga, note by note. He played Rag Pooriya. He used *meend* perfectly, and had full control of his *saaz* and rhythm. He is a disciple of Pt. Ravi Shankar ji. Another noted sitarist who gave a performance was Ustaad Imrat Khan. He has no match for his *Jor-Jhala*. He plays *gayaki ang* in his performances. The culture of the *Gharana* through his Imdad Khani touches was never before seen.

- **Shujaat Hussain Khan,** Rose Garden, Kala Bhawan, Sector 16, Chandigarh, February 1993—He plays *Gayaki-ang. Meend* work is perfect. He can produce seven *swaras* in one stroke of *mizraab,* which is a rare distinction. In his performance, he played *Raga Charu Keshi, (Karnatka Raga), (Khula Raga)* according to him. He sang when he was playing on sitar a *Bandish* of Ustaad Ameer Khan, Laj Rakho Tum Mori *gusanyian. Raga Khamaj* was also played and sung simultaneously by him as *"Man Lago Mera Yaar Faqiri Mein."*According to him, the sitar was invented by Ameer Khusro and basically it was based on *Tri tantri* veena. He believes in his own style, not in any *Gharana*, though he belongs to Imdad Khani *Gharana.*

- **Budhaditya Mukerjee,** October 27, 1995, Bhartiya Vidya Bhawan, Sector 27, Chandigarh—When asked about his style of sitar playing, the answer was quick and to the point: *"gayaki aur Tantarkari Ka Sahi Smavesh Hai."* He is from the Imdad Khani *Gharana.* He has depth of feeling and emotion and an outstanding technique, which he expresses through his music. He is a disciple of his father, Pandit Bimlendu Mukherjee, a great sitarist of Imdad Khani *Gharana.* His *meend* work and *jor jhala* are superb. He plays *gats* after presenting enthralling pieces of *alaap, jor,* and *jhala*. The soothing notes flow from the strings of the sitar like waterfalls, which makes one spellbound. His *meend* work is so beautiful that he is perfect in producing *Tar saptak's Sa swara* from *Madhya saptak's Sa.*

- **Shahid Parvez,** Tagore theatre, March 19, 1993. Chandigarh— The All India Bhaskar Rao *Nritya* and Sangeet Sammelan presented this great artist in Tagore Theatre in Chandigarh on March 19, 1993. He makes soft and delicate notes on the sitar and has mastery over the *saaz.* He can play four to five *swaras meend* in one stroke. One gets the feeling of *gayaki ang,* or we can say that he plays sitar *gats* just as shadows of *Chhota Khayal.* He plays the *tihais* with powerful *mizraab* strokes, which show his grip over rhythm.

- **Mohsin Ali Khan,** Panjab Kala Bhawan, Sector 16, Chandigarh, May 27, 1993—He belongs to Bhendi Bazaar *Gharana,* also known as Moradabadi *Gharana*. At that time, he was learning from Partho Das. He played *vilambit gat* in *Bageshwari* in *Ek-taal* and *drut* in *Teentaal* was marked by an extensive use of *meend*, which added an extremely pleasing *goonj* to the instrument. He plays an intricate *alaap*. He explores high octaves more than the lower ones. He shows the virtuosity with the *jhala* on the instrument. His playing is soft, and pleasing notes are good to the ear marked by the highs and lows, which prevent his recital from becoming repetitive.

- **Ustaad Vilayat Khan,** Bhartiya Vidya Bhawan, Sector 16, Chandigarh, October 21, 1994 (organized by Indian National Theatre)—He played *Rag Bhairavi* and deviated into other ragas by shifting the key note and created the atmosphere of *rag Khamaj, Tilang, Peelu, Jai Jaiwanti, Nand,* and then again returned to *Bhairavi.* The changing of raga was done with such a subtle smoothness that it seemed comparable to the smooth changing of lines by a train where not a slight bump is felt. He plays *alaap, vilambit gat,* drut with *taans,* and lastly *jhala.* He handles and explores the sitar, making it sing. He has the command and dexterity of the fingers so that each stroke is powerful yet fine-tuned and controlled. His *Jhala* seems like a bunch of waves coming toward you. He is the one who added a new dimension to the sitar by introducing the *gayaki ang.* It was the natural outcome to one who was taught the *surbahar,* the sitar, and vocal music all at the same time. He follows the purest form of classical music.

- **Debu Prasad Chakarvarty,** Tagore Theater Chandigarh, April 7, 1994 (organized by Pracheen Kala Kendra)—He has learned this art from Ajay Sinha Roy of the Senia *Gharana.* He played Raga Yaman Kalyaan, starting with *alaap* to a composition in *madhya laya* before going to a wonderful *drut gat.* The complete mastery of the structure and the enlivening *layakari* are the qualities he has preserved. During the fast *gat,* the *taan* patterns were rapid, but even then, the sitar and tabla playing were perfectly balanced. The coordination was absolutely natural without the display of acrobatics. During the fast *gat,* the *taan* patterns were rapid and the tabla and sitar playing were perfectly balanced. He used the technique of *mizraab* playing in the *Jhala* through heavy and light strokes, bringing out perfect clarity of notes.

- **Dr. Saroj Ghosh,** A disciple of Ustaad Amjad Ali Khan Sahib and plays her sitar mixed with sarod techniques.
- **Piare Lal,** Ektara player, Maloya Colony, U. T. Chandigarh, November 11, 1992—A Kabir *panthi* by religion, he is a musician in himself. He told me that the *Ektara* is the base of all stringed instruments. He played three *bhajans* and classical *ghazal* tunes and film songs (with some music also) on only one string. He has great control over the *swaras*. He makes his instruments himself. Only Piyali or the little gourd is ordered from the pot maker. Then the *bamboo stick, baint*, and *gaj* are needed. It is played with a bow.
- **Pt. Gopal Krishan,** Veena player—He believes that veena techniques have been adopted by sitar players and some of the techniques of the sitar have been adopted by veena players. He has perfection in *Alaap*.
- **Salil Shankar,** All India Bhaskar Rao Sangeet Sammelan, November 28, 1986, Tagore Theatre A disciple of Pt. Ravi Shankar ji, he is at his best when he plays the fast *gats*. He played Raga Bhimplasi with *alaap, jor, jhala*, and then *Vilambit gat* followed by *Drut gat*. He played a pleasant tune in raga Mishra Khamaj, which had the beauty of *guyaki ang*. He makes full use of all the strings of the instrument while playing.
- **Arvind Parikh,** Sangeet 1968, August, p. 55.—Shri Arvind Parikh learned sitar from Ustaad Vilayat Khan. Arvind ji plays devotional songs and tunes on sitar. Ustaad Vilayat Khan taught him all his own as well as Ustaad Inayat Khan's sitar *vaadan* style with full devotion.
  Arvind Parikh was born on Oct 19, 1927, in Ahmadabad. His mother was a talented lady with whose inspiration Arvind got the heights of sitar playing. His father Sh. Govardhan Das was also a great musician and sitar player. Arvind ji learnt sitar *vaadan* from Shri Makrand Badshah and then from Ustaad Vilayat Khan. His *vaadan* shally had gayaki-*ang* which has been adopted by the present artists like Shujat Hussain Khan. Arvind Parikh's *vaadan* shally had the sweetness of sound and clearance of *swaras*.

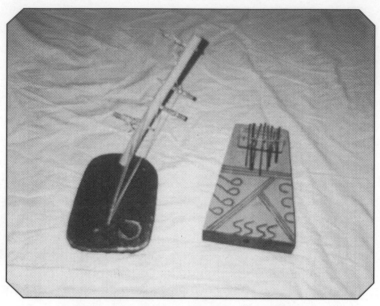

Four stringed, no name (from Thailand)
Five stringed from Tanzania (placed on a wooden piece)

Six-stringed Ukulele (from Russia)

Two-stringed Koto (from Japan)

Four-stringed Banjo (from Canada)

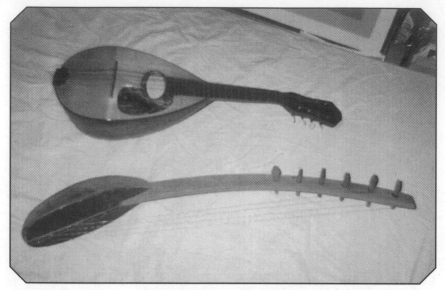

Eight-stringed Mandolin

Three-stringed Keshmat (from Turkey)

Four-stringed Guitar (from Phillipines)

Sitting position with sitar

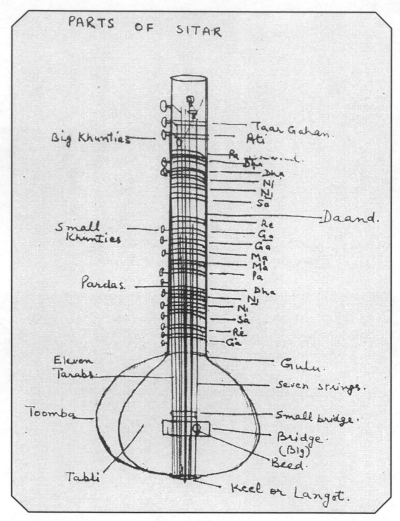

Parts of the sitar

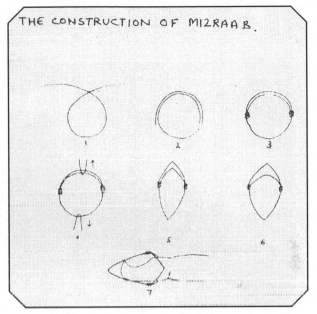

Construction and wearing of plectrum/mizraab

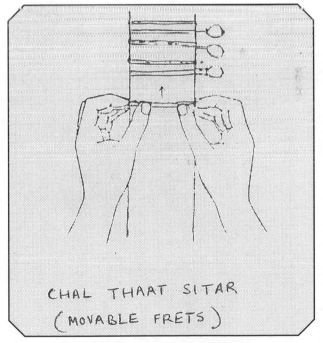

Chal thaat sitar/movable frets

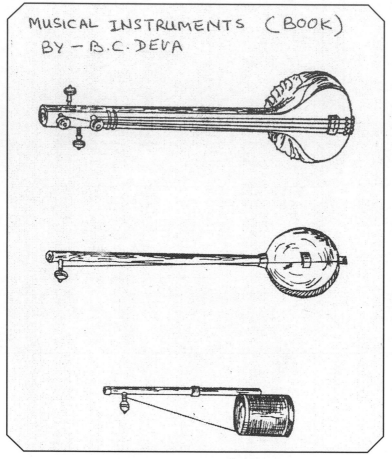

Musical instruments

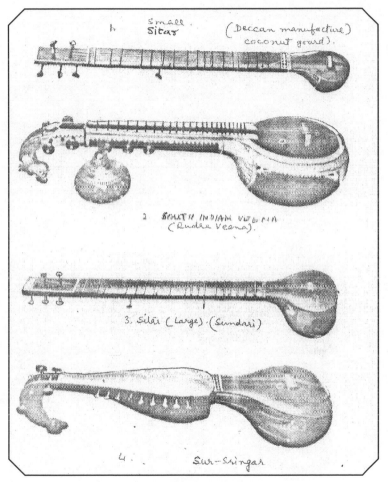

1. Small Sitar (Deccan manufacture) (coconut gourd).

2. SOUTH INDIAN VEENA ('Rudra Veena').

3. Sitar (Large) (Sundari)

4. Sur-Sringar

Stringed instruments

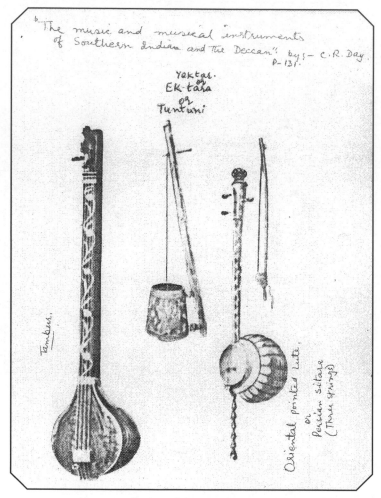

Stringed instruments

GLOSSARY

Akarsh: Inside stroke on sitar's first string with plectrum. It is also called "da."

Achal: Where the notes are fixed, a sitar with all the frets needed for lower, middle, and high notes.

Achal thaat: Where the notes are fixed in achal thaat sitars.

Alaap: It is an expression of the characteristics of the raga. Alaap has no measured rhythm and is very slow in tempo. It is the beginning of a musical composition.

Ang: Limb or body. In music: a scale. A scale consists of two angas; purwanga-(Sa, Re, Ga, Ma,) and uttranga (Pa, Dha, Ni, and the next higher Sa).

Antra: The second part of the song/composition in high notes is called antra.

Anudaat: This tone, an "unraised tone," was used in singing or reciting of Rig-Veda mantras.

Anustupa: Anustupa is the name for a chhand and a chhand is a style of singing. Every Anustupa chhand has four parts and every part has eight swaras, so there are thirty two swaras in total in an Anustupa chhand. This tradition of singing the vedic chants is continued till today.

Apkarsh: Outside stroke on sitar's first string with plectrum. It is also called "ra."

Aroh: The ascending notes are called Aroh (i.e., Sa, Re, Ga, Ma, Pa, Dha, Ni, Sa.)

Ati: a small bridge on the neck of the sitar, where the strings are kept.

Atodhya vidhi: Name of the process in which Bharat described the human body as physical veena, in which vocal chords work like strings.

Avroh: The descending notes are known as Avroh (i.e., Sa, Ni, Dha, Pa, Ma, Ga, Re, Sa).

Baaj ka taar: First string of sitar from outside.

Bandish: Fixed vocal or instrumental composition, bound by a rhythmic cycle.

Bhajan: A devotional song.

Bhava: Expression.

Bol: The name of a stroke of mizraab on sitar string is called "bol," as Da, Dir, Da, Ra, etc.

Chal Thaat: When we can move the frets on the sitar.

Cheez: Fixed song composition, like bandish.

Chikari: A stroke of plectrum, on last string of the sitar. It is the name also given to the last string of the sitar from outside to inside.

Daand: Neck or lute of the sitar.

Darh: Small post made of antelope horn that is inserted into the daand of the sitar, to support the Chikari string. The name of the last string is chikari.

Dhamar: It is a composition with fourteen beats, also called Hori Dhamar.

Dhrupad: It is made of two words—Dhruv and Pada. "Dhruv" means definite and "Pada" means fixed, so it is a definite and fixed style of compositions. The text of the dhrupad is in a dilect of Hindi and is in praise of gods and kings.

Drut: It is the name of speed, used for fast gats with fast rhythm or beat.

Gaan: A Sanskrit word used for vocal singing.

Gandhaar gram: The scale which begins with Ga.

Gandharva: One who belongs to a semi divine class of beings, a heavenly or celestial singer.

Gandharva music: A kind of music which was said to please the gods. Vedic music represents Gandharva music.

Gamak: A particular ornament or embellishment used in Indian music. It is an essential part of the melodic structure. It is produced by touching two notes together.

Garanth: A historical religious book.

Gat: A fixed instrumental composition in any tala or tempo.

Gatha: This word means: a story.

Gayan: This word is used for vocal singing.

Gayatri: In vedic period, this was the name of the style of singing. It is also the name of the Goddess Gayatri.

Geeti: Song of an ancient origin.

Gharana: A family tradition from one family through succeeding generations.

Gharanedaar: A traditional music composition.

Ghaseet: Pulling the string from one note to the next and back again in rapid succession.

Ghazal: This is a light classical romantic composition in Urdu language.

Gram: This word is used for scale. There were three grams prevalent in ancient periods—shadaj gram, madhyam gram, and gandhaar gram—but now only shadaj gram and madhyam gram are in use.

Greh swara: The note which is set in the beginning of a raga or composition.

Gulu: The place where the guard and neck of the sitar are joined together.

Guru: Teacher, spiritual guide, master and preceptor.

Gurumukhi: The name of a language.

Jamjama: When two notes are repeated two times together.

Jawari: It is the bridge of the sitar and is also called Ghurch. We put strings on it.

Jhala: This is the third part of a raga, after the gat, increasing speed and excitement, ending with a climax, beautifying the mode.

Jhankar: Vibration.

Jore ke taar: These are second and third strings of the sitar from the outside.

Kachua: Tortoise.

Kala: Art work.

Kampan: Vibration.

Kan swara: To touch a note softly.

Khayal: Literally, meaning is imagination. It was invented by Amir Khusro in the thirteenth century. It is a vocal style of Indian classical music.

Khunti: Peg.

Komal: Flat notes.

Krintan: When we touch two to three notes swiftly and then take the fingers away, but the notes keep the relation.

Lakshan geet: When a song is sung with a description of the notes.

Langot: The place where the strings are tied.

Laukik music: Post-Vedic music.

Lok geet: A folk song.

Madhyam gram: The scale starting with Ma note.

Mahabharata: One of the two Indian epics.

Mandra saptak: Lower notes.

Mantras: Devotional, poetic lines.

Matra: It is a metrical beat.

Meend work: Stretching of string to produce another note, connecting the sounds using microtones.

Meru: The place where the taar gahan is fitted.

Mishrit ragas: Mixed modes to create beauty and newness.

Mizraab: Plectrum made of wire, to strike on strings to play sitar.

Murki: Fast playing of two notes, one after another, and again coming to the previous note.

Nakhi: Plectrum.

Nritya: Dance.

Nayaki: Main string or *baaj* ka taar.

Nayas: This is the note where the composition finishes.

Nayika: Plectrum.

Paniniya Shiksha: Name of the book.

Parda: Fret.

Prampara: Tradition.

Pukaar: When two notes are touched together.

Pustak Dharini: The goddess of knowledge.

Raga: A raga is a melodious composition having its own characteristics which distinguish it from other ragas.

Ramayan: One of the two great Indian epics written by Rishi Valmiki. It is the Hindu's sacred book.

Rasas: Sentiments.

Rig-Veda: One of the four basic Vedas of Indian culture.

Rishi: A saint of scholarly nature.

Sam: It is the most important beat of the tala, which shows the tabla players and the instrumentalists coordination.

Sam-Veda: One of the four basic Vedas of Indian culture.

Sangeet: Good music.

Sangeetacharya: Music teacher.

Saptak: It comprises seven notes of Indian music. It is called Octave also.

Sarvottam: Best.

Senia: Name of the tradition.

Shailie: Technique.

Shadaj: Name of the first note (Sa).

Shadaj gram: The scale which starts with the note Sa.

Shishya: Student.

Shruti: Indian music has twenty-two shruties or microtones.

Shudh swara: Natural note.

Sooksham: Smallest.

Soot: Rolling over the notes swiftly to reach another note, without producing any sound of in between notes.

Sthai: Constant.

Sundaries: Frets.

Swara: Tone of definite pitch, note or syllable.

Swarit: The ancient swara between the pitches of Udaata and Anudaat.

Swroop: Shape.

Taar saptak: High pitch notes.

Tabli: The cover of the guard.

Tala: The Indian music is based on rhythm or tala cycle.

Tappa: It is a kind of music from Punjab, India, which is sung in a fast laya and has two parts: sthai and antra.

Tarana: It is a composition of some words which actually has no meaning, but is sung in rhythm. Tarana has sthai and antra and is good for entertainment.

Thumri: It is a composition with fewer words and is usually sung in teen tala.

Tihai or Tiya: The ending notes of a taan or toraa.

Tivra note: Sharp note.

Toraa or Taan: These are illustrations which are of many types—spat taan, vakra taan, koot taan, etc.

Tukra: A piece of composition.

Udaat: Raised tone referring to Vedic swaras.

Upadhi: Honor.

Upnishads: Religious epics.

Vaadak: Instrument player.

Vaadan: Playing of an instrument.

Vaadan shailies: Playing techniques of an instrument.

Vaanies: Style of singing in ancient times was called vaanies

Varjit swara: Abandoned note.

Vedic: Vedic music.

Veena: Name of the instrument.

Vidhya: Knowledge.

Vilambit: Slow tempo.

Vistaar: Elaboration of the raga or expansion.

Yug: Time period.

ENGLISH NAMES OF THE NOTES

1. *Sa* — Tonic
2. *Re* — Semitone
3. *Re* — Major tone or super tone
4. *Ga* — Minor third
5. *Ga* — Major third or Mediant
6. *Ma* — Fourth or sub dominant
7. *Ma* — Augmented fourth
8. *Pa* — Fifth or dominant
9. *Dha* — Minor sixth
10. *Dha* — Major sixth or submediant
11. *Ni* — Minor seventh
12. *Ni* — Major seventh or leading note
13. *Sa* — Octave or tonic

UNIVERSITIES VISITED

1. Panjab University, Chandigarh, India
2. Panjabi University, Patiala, India
3. Himachal University, Shimla, India
4. Haryana University, Rohtak, India
5. Kurukshetra University, India
6. Delhi University and Mandi House, India
7. Saskatoon University, Canada, Music Department
8. Calgary University, Canada, Music Department
9. City College, New York, USA
10. American Museum of Natural History, New York

WORKSHOPS VISITED

1. Shimla Music House, Sector 27, Chandigarh, India.
2. Rikhi Ram, Musical Instruments, 8 Marina Arcade, New Delhi, India.
3. Amrit Music Store, Sector 15, Chandigarh, India.

INTERVIEWS

1. Pt. Uma Shankar Mishra, Panjab University, Chandigarh, India.
2. Pt. Gopal Krishan, veena vaadak, Eng. Auditorium, P. U. Chandigarh, India.
3. Shujaat Hussain Khan - Sitar player, Kala Bhawan-Rose Garden, February 1993, Chandigarh.
4. Peter Van Gilder at Canada, January 1994. Pt. Ravi Shankar ji's disciple in USA.
5. Dr.David Kaplin in Saskatoon university, Canada, January 1994.
6. Dr. House in Saskatoon, Canada, January 1994.
7. Naushad Sahib (Interview on TV).
8. Budha Ditya Mukherjee, Sitarist from Bhilai, Bhartiya Vidya Bhawan, Sector 27, October 28, 1995, Chandgiarh (UT).
9. Dr. Saroj Ghosh, PU, Chandigarh, India, 1997.
10. Dr. Narender Singh Virdi (I attended one seminar on music in Chandigarh with him).
11. Late Dr. Sagar Pandit. (My Guru, Disciple of Late Pt. Omkar Nath Thakur).
12. Debaparsad Chakarborty, sitarist from Patiala *Gharana,* Sangeet Sammelan - Tagore Theatre. April 7, 1994.
13. Ustaad Vilayat Khan, Bhartiya Vidya Bhawan, Sector 27. October 21, 1994.
14. Shahid Parvez - Harballabh Sangeet Sammelan Devi Talab - Jallandhar, December 27, 1993.
15. Mr. Piarc Lal - Ektara Player from Haryana, Kabir Panthi, 11, 11-95. (Lives in Maloya, UT, Chandigarh).
16. Shri Viram Jasani Sitar Player. Harballabh Sangeet Sammelan, September 28, 1990. He played Raga Bageshwari.

BIBLIOGRAPHY

AUTHOR	BOOK AND PUBLICATION
Ahobal Pandit	SANGEET PARIZAT
	Sangeet Karyalya Hathras, 1971.
Allami Abul Fazal	AINE AKBARI
	1598.
Avasthy, S. S.	A CRITIQUE OF HINDUSTANI MUSIC
	Dhanpat Rai, Jallandhar.
Brahaspati Acharya	BHARTIYA SANGEET KE ITIHAS KA PRACHEEN KAAL
Bhatt Vishambhar Nath	SANGEET ARCHNA
	1958.
Bandopadhyaya S.	MUSIC OF INDIA
Bhatkhande	A SHORT HISTORICAL SURVEY OF
Pt. Vishnu Narayan	THE MUSIC OF UPPER INDIA BHATKHANDE SANGEET SHASTRA
	Sangeet Karyalya Hathras, 1958.
	HINDUSTANI SANGEET PADWATI
	Sangeet Karyalya Hathras.
	SWARA MALIKA
	Sangeet Karyalaya Hatras, 1958.
Bharat Muni	NATYA SHASTRA
	Part IV, Oriental Institute Baroda.
Brihaspati	BHARAT KA SANGEET SIDDHANT
Kailash Chander	Shakha Soochna Vibhag, U. P.
Chaudhary, Dev Vratta	SITAR AND ITS TECHNIQUES

Chakarwarti, Dr. Indrani	SWARA AUR RAGON KE VIKAS MEIN VADHYON KA YOGDAAN
Chaudhary, Vimal Kant Rai	BHARTIYA SANGEET
	Bhartiya Gianpeeth Parkashan, New Delhi 1975.
Chunni Lal	ASHAT CHHAP KE VADHYA YANTRA
	Akhil Bhartiya Braj Sahitya Mandal, Mathura 1956.
Chaube, Dr. Sushil Kumar	HAMARA ADHUNIK SANGEET
Conran Michaal	NATIONAL MUSIC OF IRELAND 1846.
Day, C. R.	THE MUSIC AND MUSICAL INSTRUMENTS OF DECAN
Damodar Pandit	SANGEET DARPAN
	Sangeet Karyalya Hathras (UP) 1975.
Deva, B. C.	AN INFORMATION TO INDIAN MUSIC
	Publication division, ND, 1973.
	INDIAN MUSIC
	Indian Council for Cultural relations, New Delhi, 1974.
	MUSICAL INSTRUMENTS
	National Book Trust of India, New Delhi, 1977.
Daniel Anail	INTRODUCTION TO THE STUDY OF MUSICAL SCALES
Felber Ervin	THE INDIAN MUSIC OF THE VEDIC AND THE CLASSICAL PERIOD
Fakeerullah Saifudin	RAG DARPAN, 1663.
Govardhan, Shanti	SANGEET SHASTRA DARPAN, 1966
Garg, Laxmi Narayan	HAMARE SANGEET RATAN
Garg, Prabhu Lal	SANGEET SAGAR
	Sangeet Karyalya Hathras, 1960.
Gupta, Anil	MUSIC OF INDIA
	Rangulf Club road, Calcutta-33.
Ghosh Nikhil	FUNDAMENTAL OF RAGA AND TALA

	WITH A NEW SYSTEM OF NOTATION
Joshi Umesh	BHARTIYA SANGEET KA ITIHAS
	Mansarover Prakashan Mahal, Regozabad
	(UP) 1957.
Jones Sir William	THE MUSICAL INSTRUMENTS
Jain Bhanu Kumar	BHARTIYA SANGEET MEIN TANTU
	VADHYA
Junious Menfred	THE SITAR
Khan, Mobarak Hussain	MUSIC AND ITS STUDY
Kulshreshta,	THEORY OF INDIAN MUSIC
Jagdish Sahaye	
Khusro Ameer	DAWALRANI KHIJRI
Lalit, Prof. Kishore Singh	DHWANI AUR SANGEET
	Bhartiya Gianpeeth Prakashan, New
	Delhi, 1977.
Madaan Panna Lal	TEACHING OF MUSIC BHARTIYA
	SANGEET AUR USKA VIKAS
	1965.
Maankaran Veena	SANGEET SAAR
	Bhartiya Gian Peeth Prakashan, ND
	1986.
Ministry of information	FACTS ABOUT INDIA
and broadcasting	1960.
Matang	BRAHDESHISKH 1976.
Matasyavacharya	RIGVEDADA SANHITA
	Chukhamba Sanskrit Series, Banaras,
	1965.
Mishr Dr. Lal Mani	TANTRI NAAD (PART I)
	BHARTIYA SANGEET VADHYA
	Gianpeeth Prakashan, ND 1975.
Nanya Dev	BHARAT BHAVYAM (PART I)
	Indira Kala Vishwa Vidhalya Kheragarh.
Naarad	NARDIYA SHIKSHA
	SANGEET MAKRAND
Parikh Arvind	SITAR AUR USKA VIKAS
	1968.
Paathak,	PRAVEEN PRASHAN PANJIKA
Pt. Jagdish Narayan	1970

	SANGEET SHASTRA MIMANSA (PART I) 1965.
	SANGEET NIBANDH MALA
	SANGEET SHASTRA PRAVEEN SKH 1967.
Popley, H. A.	MUSIC OF INDIA
Pranjpay	BHARTIYA SANGEET KA ITIHAS
Raghunath Pt.	SANGEET SUDHA
Ravi Shankar, Pandit	Pt. RAVI SHANKAR KE ORCHESTRA
	Sangeet Karyalya Hathras, UP (1986).
	MY MUSIC MY LIFE
Sen Sharmistha	THE STRING INSTRUMENTS OF NORTH INDIA
Sarkar Debashish	QUIZ ON INDIAN MUSIC AND DANCE
Saxena, Dr. Kumari Madhubala	KHAYAL SHAILY KA VIKAS
Swami Prajna Nanda	HISTORICAL DEVELOPMENT OF INDIAN MUSIC
Stephen M. Slawek	SITAR TECHNIQUES IN NIBADHA FORM
Sharma Amal Das	VISHVA SANGEET KA ITIHAS
Saxena, S. K.	AESTHETICAL ESSAYS
	Chanakya Publication, New Delhi, 1981.
Sharangdev Pandit	SANGEET RATNAKAR
	Rangulf Club Road, Calcutta—33.
Shastri K. Vasudev	SANGEET SHASTRA
	Hindi Smiti Soochna Vibhag Lucknow, UP, 1968.
Swami Pratap	SANGEET SAAR
Singh Maharaja	Sangeet Karyalya, Hathras UP, 1976.
Sharma,	SITAR MALIKA
Shri Bhagawat Saran	
Suri, Harinayak	SANGEET SAAR
Tagore, S. M.	HINDU MUSIC
	Chaukhamba Sanskrit Series Varanasi, 1965.

	THE MUSIC OF INSTRUMENTS OF HINDUS CSS, Varanasi, 1956. THE STORY OF MUSICAL INSTRUMENT CSS, Varanasi, 1968.
Tara Singh Prof.	VAADAN KALA Punjabi University, Patiala, 1972.
Thakur, Late	PRANAV BHARTI
Pt. Omkar Nath -	Kashi Hindu Vishwa Vidhalaya, Varanasi, 1956. SANGEETANJALI KHVV, Varanasi, 1958
Virdi, Narender Singh	SANGEET ATE USDI GURBANI VICH MAHATTATA Modern Sahitya Academy, Amritsar.
Vasant	SANGEET VISHARAD
Vandopadhayaya	MUSICAL INSTRUMENTS OF INDIA
Shripad	Chaukhamba Orientalia Varanasi, 1980
Vishnu Das	SARGAM Marg Publication, 1977.
Vidya Vilasi Pandit	VADHYA PRAKASH Encyclopedia Britannica, volume 16

PERIODICALS

1. Sangeet Bilawal Ank - January 1953.
2. Sangeet Kalyan Ank - January 1954.
3. Sangeet Bhairav Ank - January 1955.
4. Sangeet Kafi Ank - January 1958.
5. Sangeet Karyalya Hathras.5. Sangeet, Ank, January 1961.
6. Sangeetika - Sangeet Sadan Prakashan, South Malaka - Allahabad - January 1975.
7. Vadhya Vaadan - Ibid.
8. Sangeet, Sangeet Karyalaya Hathras - 1968.
9. Sitar Shiksha, Sangeet Karyala Hathras - 1968.

INDEX

bold page numbers denote photos and illustrations

Ameer Khusro/Amir Khusro, 17,
    24–26, 28, 30, 36, 74, 123
Amrat Kundali, 14
Amrit Sen/Amritsen/Imratsen, 52, 54,
    56, 57, 60, 64, 75, 80, 82, 83, 86
Analambi veena, 14, 18
antelope horn, 41, 42, 43
antra, 7, 58, 59, 61, 64, 67, 111
anudaat, 12, 32, 111
Anumandra Alaapchaari, 58
anustupa (meter), 5, 111
Apkarsh, 45, 111
Arabs, 3, 20, 23
Aroh, 39, 111
Arvind Parikh, 84, 101
Ashiq Ali Khan/Ashique Ali Khan,
    59, 83
Assam, 42
Atharva Veda, 4
Ati (pacisa), 42, 112
Ati mandra Ma Ga Re Sa, 40
Ati mandra Ni Dha Pa, 40
Ati mandra Pancham, 40
Ati mandra shadaj, 40
Atiswara, 5, 12, 33
atodhya vidhi, 3, 112
Aurangzeb, 27
avandh vadhyas, 11
Avroh, 39, 112
Avtaar, 57

B

baaj (style), 79
Baaj Ka Taar/Baaj Ki Taar, 37, 38, 40,
    43, 112
baaj string, 37
baaj vidhies, 79

Babu Ishwari Prasad, 48, 81
Babu Khan, 59, 82, 85
Bahadur Khan, 48, 74, 75, 81
Baiju Bawra, 28
balalaika, 21
balancing circumflex register notes
    (*swarit*), 5
Bandish (tune), 59, 60, 65, 67, 95, 112
banjo, **103**
Barkat Ali Khan/Barkatulla Khan/
    Barktullah Khan, 48, 81–83
Baroda, 82
bass register (*Mandra*), 5
Batta been, 15
bead (*manka*), 43
beat (*matra*), 45, 57–60, 69, 115
been, 11, 28, 29, 74
been shaily, 60
beenkaars, 80, 81
beenkari ang, 83
bella/bela, 11
bells, metal, 11
Bhairavi, 48
bhajans, 7, 53, 60, 112
Bharat, 3, 6, 10, 18
Bharat, Maharishi, 15
Bhartiya Sangeet, 25
Bhartiya Sangeet Aur Uska Vikas, 31
*Bhartiya Sangeet Ke Itihas Ka Pracheen
    Kaal* (Acharya Brahaspati), 18,
    121
*Bhartiya Sangeet Mein Tantoo
    Vadhya*, 44
Bhartiya Sangeet Vadhya, 43
Bhatkhande notation system, 95
bhavas (rasas), 40, 112
Bhayankar ras, 8
Bhilai, 84

Kaplan, David, 21
Karimdad Khan, 76
Karnataka Academy of Music, 15
kartal, 11
Kartik Kumar, 96
Karuna ras, 8
kashat-trang/kasht-tarang, 11
Kashi, 81
Kathak Samhitas (Manu samriti granth), 13
kcel (*longorus, lagot*), 41
kehrawa, 7
keshmat, **104**
khali, 70
Khamaj, 48
Khan (Gulaam), 82
Khandaan, 80
Khandaani cheez, 80
Khuruj, 56
Kharaj ki Taar, 38, 43
khatka, 8, 91
khayal (light music), 7–8, 53, 57, 80, 95, 114
khayal ang, 58
khayal gayaki, 53, 54, 59, 60, 91
Khayal Gayan *shaily*, 64
khayal shaily, 53, 60
Khayal style, 91
khayal-ang-in, 83
khunties, 42, 43, 114
Khushaal Khan, 27
Khusro Khan, 26, 27–28
Khusro Malik, 25, 26
kinnari veena, 14–15, 21, 22, 25
Kinnor, 21
komal (flat note), 69, 114
komal Ni, 39
koormi veena, 15

koto, **103**
Kramatulla Khan, 84
Kramik Pustak Malika (Vishnu Naraya Bhaat Khande), 73
krintan, 65, 70, 91, 114
Kripa, 27
Krishan Rav, Sh., 76
krushtha/krusta, 5, 12, 33
kubzika veena, 15
Kush, 14
kush-tar-kar, 21
Kut-baj *gat shaily*, 63–64
Kutbuddin Khilji, 27

L

Lal Mani Misar, 43
Lalit Khan, 82
langot (*longorus*, keel), 41, 43, 114
Laraj ki taar, 43
Lav, 14
laya, 57, 81
Laykaari, 81
light music (*khayal*), 7–8, 53, 57, 80, 95, 114
lok geets, 53, 114
longorus (*langot*, keel), 41
Lono-Koto, 20
Lucknow, 56, 57, 60, 81, 82
lute, 20
lyre, 13, 20

M

Ma, 4, 5, 12, 32, 118
Madhayam gram, 33
Madhya (medium register), 5
Madhya Laya, 64

Nayas notes, 97, 115
Nemat Khan, 27
New York State Library, 19
Ni, 4, 5, 12, 32, 118
Ni Shudh, 39
Nihalsen, 52, 56, 57, 75, 83
Nikhil Banerji/Nikhil Benerjee, 91, 96
nineteenth-century musical trends,
    37, 42, 46–48, 52–56, 58–60,
    61–62, 64, 75–76, 82, 94
ninth-century musical trends, 14
Nishaad, 12, 13
Nishaat Hussain Khan/Nishaat Khan,
    84, 96
Nishad, 4
NOM TOM Ka Alap, 48
North America, instruments in, 21
not raised register notes (*Anudata*), 5
notation symbols, 68–74
notation system, 95
nritya, 1, 2, 115
nritya shailies, 79
nuts (pegs), 43

O

octaves, 33, 40, 69
Omkar Nath, Pt./Omkar Nath
    Thakur, Pt., 25, 30
ornamentation, 43

P

Pa, 4, 5, 12, 32, 118
Paathak, Pt. Jagdish Narayan, 57
pacisa (*Ati*), 42
pakhawaj, 11, 52, 56
Palestine, instruments in, 21

Pan Khan, 48, 75, 81
Pancham, 4, 12, 13, 33
Panini, 3, 13
Paniniya Shiksha, Shalok No. 12, 13, 115
Panna Lal Vijpayi/Panna Lal Vijpeyi,
    48, 81
Panna Lall Madan, 31
papaya string, 37
papeeha, 38
pardas (frets), 19, 42, 115. *See also*
    frets (*pardas*)
Parikh Arvind, 31, 123
patriotic songs, 7
patronage, 9, 80, 81, 83
pause (rest), 69
peacock fiddle (*Mayuri*), 21, 23
pegs (nuts), 43
Persia, instruments in, 21, 23, 24
Persians, 3
Philippines, instruments in, **105**
piano, 11
Piare Lal, 101
pichhora, 13
Pilu, 48
pitches, 5
playing position, 44
plectrum (bow) (*mizraab*), 11, 19, 20,
    21, 44–45, **107**. *See also mizraab*
    (plectrum)
poongi, 11
Poorvi Baaj, 57
Popley, H. A., 17, 22, 28, 124
Prajnanada/Swami Prajna Nanda
    (Swami), 1, 12, 124
Prampara, 78, 115
Prathama/Prathma, 5, 12, 32
Pre-*Gat* Period, 51, 52
pukar/pukaar, 71, 115

S

V

vaadak (player), 15, 19, 117
vaadan, 2, 6, 54, 58, 117
vaadan shailies
  analytical study of changing,
    56–61
  changes in, 64
  defined, 79, 117
  and historical development of sitar,
    51–55
vaadi swara, 56
vaan, 12, 13
vaani/vaanis/vaanies, 79, 80, 117
Vac-a-tat, 21
vadhya, 1
Vadhya Parkash (Vidya Vilasi Pandit),
    14, 15, 125
vadini, 48
Vaheed Khan, 84
van, 12
vana, 12
Vansh, 84
Varjit, 40
Vasant, 36, 37, 125
Vazeer Khan, 76
Vedas, 3, 9. *See also specific Vedas*
Vedic meters, 5
Vedic period, 12
Vedic sangeet, 3
veena *pustak dharini*, 3
veena vaadan, 13, 65
veena/veenas. *See also specific veenas*
  defined, 10, 117
  modification of old ones, 18–19
  Narad as inventor of, 3
Veer ras, 8
Venah/Venrah, 21

venu, 12
Vibhatsa ras, 8
vichitra veena, 19, 65, 91
vidhi, 79
Vidya Vilasi Pandit, 14, 15, 125
Vidyas, 9
Vilambit gats, 7, 53, 54, 57, 58, 59,
  60, 96
vilambit khayal, 53
vilambit teen talas, 81
Vilas Khan, 75
Vilayat Khan, 56, 58, 59, 76, 84, 91,
  96, 100
vipanchi veena, 10, 13, 16, 18
Virdi, Nirender Singh, 91
Vishambar Nath Bhatt, 31
Vishnu Digamber Pulaskar, Pt., 94
Vishnu Naraya Bhaat Khande, Pt./
  Vishnu Narayan Bhatkhande, Pt.,
  68, 73, 94–95
Vishnupur *Gharana*, 82
Vishva Sangeet Ka Itihas (Amal Dash
  Sharma), 2, 19, 20
Visram Khan, 27
vitat vadhyas, 11
vocal music
  classification of, 7
  as part of sangeet, 1
  and *vaadan shaily*, 79

W

Wahid Khan, 82
Western countries, appreciation for
  sitar, 97, 98

Y

Yajur Veda, 5
Yantra, 18
Yantra Kshetra Deepika (Tagore), 25
Yusuf Ali Khan, 59

Z

Zaafar Khani *gat shaily*, 63
Zafar Khan, 75
zamzama, 65, 71, 91
zither, 21